MW01242139

How to Give Up Golf, Please!

Publication, Press and Copyrights 2012

Dated: June 22, 2012

2nd Edition: January 1, 2014

Gayle,

You don't need to play or even know golf to appreciate that God must have a great sense of humor. Why else would He have put these characters on Earth for our entertainment?

I even took aim at my own family in this one.

Love
Cousin Wayne

How to Give Up Golf, Please!

By

Wayne J. Martin

Disclaimer

This book is about real experiences and real language as it is spoken. There is some profanity just as you would find in the unsheltered real world of golf.

The book is based, in part, upon actual events, persons, and other entities. The characters, incidents and entities portrayed and the names used herein are fictitious. Any similarity of those fictitious characters, incidents, organizations or other entities to the name attributes or actual background of any actual person, living or dead, or to any existing entity, is entirely coincidental, and unintentional unless otherwise authorized.

Dedication

For all those who have to play with

"'Characters"

And to my wife Stephanie,

Who has to live with one.

Foreword

There is so much humor to be found in this game that I did not have to make up any. There is something about golf that surfaces the true character. A game of eighteen holes is too long to hide the innermost self. And when it gets its ugliest your actions define who you really are. So lacking the proper Hallmark card for these occasions, we offer this book.

If you are buying this as a gift you might wish to get a highlighter ready. If you *received* this as a gift, please pay attention to the highlighted sections. If you are reading this for the humor, well then, that is even better.

I would be remiss if I did not quote the famous golf pro, Jimmy Demaret, who once gave advice to a struggling golfer,

"Take two weeks off – then quit the game."

Table of Contents

(I added this for highlighting convenience)

v

1: Set Low Goals

Some thoughts come from your heart and some come from your ass; but it is your brain that makes the final decision. After a few bad choices the brain learns not to listen to the ass and grows up. Some take longer than others; some never get it. All of us have to go through a few bad choices in the learning process. This teaching starts at a very early age.

If You Only Knew Jack

My mom told me that she was not making fudge even though the smell from the kitchen said otherwise. I must have done something bad as usual. So I waited a bit and slipped passed her as she watched TV. I followed the scent through the dining room in my bare feet. An Indian can walk through the woods without making a sound, I had learned. I was toes-first careful with every step. There was that one tattle-tale board on the oak floor and it was easy to spot. It was lighter than the rest as we all avoided it. I Indianed my way passed it into the kitchen.

At 3 years old I could capture all of the action without crouching. I viewed the world perfectly at an eye level few others could see. There on our white gas stove I could see the blue and yellow tongues licking at the bottom of that silver pot. I was afraid those flames might eat all of that wonderful fudge. It could happen. My mom had put up water the day before. She said that she had left it too long and showed me the empty pot.

"Now I'll have to start all over." She had said.

If that happened to the fudge that she worked so hard for, I'd never forgive myself.

The pleasing scent of bubbling chocolate was proof that it was fudge alright. I needed to be sure there was some left. I grabbed the handle and started to upend the pot to see how much was inside.

"Don't touch that, you'll burn yourself!" Mom yelled as she grabbed me and whacked me on my decision-maker.

I don't know how she got behind me so fast. Mom always seemed to be there whenever I needed her most; well maybe not always. You see, some years later, I picked up a golf club and she was not there to warn me.

First Contact

It was a Saturday and the rain was cheating me out of what should have been a perfect spring day. Even the TV antenna on the roof could not see through this much rain.

I examined the silver bullets falling from the sky and calculated the distance. I planned; planning is important even in the land of fantasy. If I ran fast then only a few drops could get me. I flew out the back door to our white clapboard garage; it was detached just like me and I got half-soaked for the effort. I wiped the rain from my arms and shook my head. Puffs of dust came up from the dry dirt floor. It hadn't rained in almost a week. Where I lived two days of rain were followed by five dry days that start on a Monday.

There was the distinct smell of the War Between the States; oil versus rust. I kicked the lawnmower with my wet sneakers and cut grass fell off in chunks. The lawnmower seemed happy for my favor and it smiled at me. Why not? The rain meant a day off for him.

There were old chains and tireless rims from bicycles long passed. They hung from the rafters like curing meat but they did nothing to break my boredom. I could swing from those rafters with a piece of clothes line but as an experienced blister recipient, I declined another attempt. I needed something newer, better to do. Desperation is surely the devil's petri dish. But then suddenly something caught my eye. My dad's golf bag appeared from nowhere!

It was safely tucked in a dry corner. As I approached, the clubs braced themselves against the unpainted wall in fear. A seven year old can be an imposing figure. I pried the frightened bag loose and grasped what I would later be told was an "'iron". An evil chill rose up from the cold ground into my heels and raced up my spine to the back of my neck. The blonde hair on my arms stood straight out and I froze as if a ghost was behind me.

Not sure that Dad would approve; I looked around to see if I was alone. I was not convinced and I could not shake the feeling of being watched. I wrapped myself in the protective blanket of my own fantasy. "I must press on for my kingdom." I unsheathed the club from the stone-colored bag and held the shaft up high, "Ah, Excalibur!" I dueled out a scene from a movie. The weight was all wrong; it was pointless. I declared it out loud as "useless"; a thought that Winston Churchill had also reached.

Golf is an accepted social activity but then so was smoking back then. Golf was simply a once a year adventure for my dad. It was something to do on vacation. It was the only sport Dad played anymore. I pulled a few balls from the lower front pocket. He must have had a great round with these. He carved some smiles on a Titleist and then on a Spalding obviously to remember the occasion.

I dropped one of the balls in front of me and took my best baseball stance. I'd smack one over Anderson's fence, their *castle walls*, and then retrieve it later. The club and my body were ready. I squared the club-face and just as I was to take my backswing, it happened. That cold chill returned to me again; it shot straight up from the floor and grabbed me on the back of the head. It yanked me backwards. My shoulders rolled upwards and a voice came so firmly and so very clear.

** Avoid frustrations and disappointments. **

I spun around, "Huh?"
**Set low goals for yourself. **

I managed to shake out a few words, "Who is this?" And then I quivered, "Where are you?"
** You don't know Jack; ah, hah, hah, hah. **

So I did what any Knight of Clapboard Castle would do, I ran back into the house and locked the door.

"Screw the kingdom!"

I had not noticed but not a single drop of rain had touched me on my return.

Straying from the Faith

Despite the objections to the contrary most people don't know Jack. Ironically they would certainly deny knowing the Jack from my garage but the truth is Jack 'is' Jack.

People believe in the internet and the guy on the radio. It is easy to believe in what you see and what you hear; but faith, as they say, is believing when you cannot. I believe the guy on the radio exists even though I wish he did not. That's not faith; that's just an opinion. The best part about the radio is the on/off switch.

** Some people need an on/off switch. **

Once you can hear Jack you're blessed with him or stuck with him. So, until you can hear Jack for yourself, I will translate. His words will be in italics between asterisks. Just because you can never get to see Jack does not mean you can't get to know him.

He has become a close friend, too close maybe. He is a conscience over my right shoulder. Jack always gets the last word and the last laugh and when he does time stops briefly, represented by a new line or even a new paragraph. Jack always tells the truth and cannot be fooled, not ever.

You might think Jack is a figment of my imagination but that is because you still don't know Jack… but you will; oh, you most definitely will.

Jack does not play golf; to entertain such a notion would be in direct violation of his own principles and teachings. I, however, strayed from the faithful and took up the game with open arms. Whenever I try to challenge Jack, he simply reminds me,

** *Don't get smart; stay the way you are!* **

Golden Shires

The comedian Lewis Black angrily shouts the absolute truth, "If you ever have an argument with a golfer you have already won because your IQ is at

LEAST… 50 points HIGHER than his. I know this
because **I…** am a golfer.". My dad played golf.

We lived in a small town called Islip on Long Island.
You may live 'in' a state or 'in' a town but you live 'on' an
island. Like golf, we don't make the rules; that's just the
way it is and we have to live 'within' the rules; some of us
anyway.

My family vacationed in New Hampshire every
August when I was of Little League age. My parents
would yank me from my Long Island baseball team to
miss the last month of the season. We won the state
championship in '61 and they went on to Williamsport,
Pennsylvania without me. I loved baseball and I hated
New Hampshire for that very reason. Everyone knew it
was not my choosing and my teammates were very
sympathetic.

"We only won because you weren't here!"

They may have been right. At age eleven, I would
have been one of the youngest and probably sat on the
bench. I would have been miserable. It all works out
though; one of the best places in the world to be eleven
and miserable is in New Hampshire. My mom found
ways to occupy my time and stick with New Hampshire-
like activities; like it or not. I blame this childhood
trauma for my willingness to stick to things too long;
things like golf and drinking, for example. I would keep
at sports to offset my lack of talent. Some of my rich
friends went to baseball camp to get better. But no

matter how much you may want something, it still might not be within your reach. This is where Jack comes in to remind us.

** Giving up is part of the learning experience. **

My dad was smaller than average, blue eyed and wiry like me except he had dark hair. He always looked like an older version of Johnny Carson. He had a good swing but he lacked lessons, practice and commitment to the game. Mostly he lacked the time and what little he had was used to play rather than practice. No one was surprised, after all, this is a man who was in the Navy in WWII and never took the time to learn how to swim. I consider my dad to be my book's first character.

It was destiny that Dad and my older brother, Bobby, would hit the links with far more balls than experience. The starter would choose some poor bastards and make them play with my family. On this day the Irish starter stuck it to some bloke from England with poor timing. They were hitting a few balls off the practice tee.

"I've never taken a lesson in my life." Dad was proud to say.

"Ah, that explains it then." The Brit sounded like Holmes who had solved a great mystery.

His name was Walter Higgins. He and his silver hair worked at and for Reader's Digest Magazine. He wore plaid shorts and his legs were whiter than two freshly painted out of bounds stakes. He was tall, too tall for the game and looked particularly awkward. His feet were too close to the ball, so he bent his butt away too compensate. From a distance he looked like something you might type by mistake, like a left parenthesis and a back slash. Don't bother, here it is:

$$(\backslash_{\text{•}}$$

For all his strange ways he managed to stripe the ball right down the middle.

"Ah, there you go." He'd color-commentate as he'd hit one after another.

My dad watched and tried to copy Mr. Higgins while I shook a bowed head. Dad slapped a few down the middle but they curved over the right field wall. It did not matter. Dad never broke 100 but he felt compelled to teach my older brother how to play.

"You put the ball on the tee, take the club back slow and hit it. After that you are not allowed to touch the ball again until it's on the green. We play it wherever it lies and we always putt everything out." The Englishman nodded in agreement.

As a golfer my brother was a solid baseball player. He had taken to lifting weights and his white golf shirt appeared two sizes too small. Bobby had forearms that were the size of my calves. A better image would be a fourteen year old Arnold; Schwarzenegger, not Palmer. He stayed muscle-bound stiff over an unsuspecting victim, a ball that was about to be murdered. Today was the anniversary of last year's killing spree. Closer would have been better but he positioned himself so far from the ball it was almost beyond his reach.

"You mean like this?"

His firm grip strangled the club head motionless. There was no waggle in this set-up. My brother would take it back slow like an executioner and then attack it from the top so the shaft would bend in mid-air. This technique, called casting, comes in very handy when fishing or beheading someone, but it is a sure disaster in a golf swing.

"Slower" Dad said not knowing how to correct the problem.

Bobby took ten practice swings before actually hitting because, as you know, repetition is the key to proper weight lifting.

My dad felt that I was still too young to play. I'd watch them hit their tee shots and take off down the first fairway. After a few dozen well-intentioned shots they would all disappear out of sight.

I would stick around the practice area to putt, chip and try their pizza. I already missed Long Island and this New England pizza almost brought me to tears. I am not sure about golf but quitting pizza in New Hampshire must be fairly common. I think it was ketchup with Velveeta on some kind of toasted flour product. They found some real oregano so they could make it smell like pizza. It was a cruel joke played on my taste buds by my very own nose. The worst part is I had had this before and ordered it again thinking it might have gotten better.

Jack's voice came out from a nearby cornfield,

*** If at first you don't succeed and try the same thing again, you're an idiot. ***

"Idiot?" I questioned. "Hey Jack, you could apply for the village position."

*** No thanks; too much competition around here. ***

My father was a bit of a masochist, in addition to aggravating himself at golf he was also a Red Sox fan; a Post-Babe Ruth Red Sox fan. I left nothing to chance so I rooted for the Yankees.

"They can beat any team with their bench players." My brother said of the Yankees. This was what my mom would call a left-handed compliment. He is a devout Catholic and loyal Braves fan.

My dad would chime in and say, "The damn Yankees stole Babe Ruth. They bought the pennant."

So enters the world of "excuses"; a required set of tools for taking up the game of golf. I needed no such excuse. If you know Jack then you can understand why I am a Yankee fan. In the 50s and 60s they ruled the game.

*** It's all about sticking with a winner; until they become losers and that's when you stick it to them."

"I guess that's why you hang with me."

*** Your low self-esteem shows good judgment on your part. ***

Knowing When to Stop

It was nearly three hours later that my dad and brother would make the turn. After nine holes of stressing out the foursome behind them they'd stop for lunch. Not everyone stopped after nine holes for lunch but I think the starter might have insisted. I would come up and join them. The Englishmen suddenly had to attend to something at home, or work or somewhere, anywhere else. My dad still had his sights on breaking 100. This means he would need 50 or less for the front nine.

"Did you bring in the scorecard? " Dad asked.

"No, I left it in the cart." My brother apologized.

"Good. At least we can enjoy our lunch."

It seemed we always ordered egg salad sandwiches on rye. My older brother would mix it up once in a while with a burger and fries. Neither one of them ever tried the pizza. I mean, how smart is that?! My brother would have two Cokes and my dad would inhale three or four beers. He would take one for the road before they headed back out. I'd knock down a chocolate-milk and chase it with a Coke on the rocks.

I was a smaller version of my dad with platinum blonde hair. My blue eyes made people play close attention to me; much closer than I really wanted. Dressed in the right clothes I could have easily passed as Dennis the Menace, except I wasn't as well-behaved. I would hang out at the practice area where every local hick would come up and show me how to chip or putt. There is no shortage of advice on the golf course.

"This is where the game is played." Some self-appointed know-it-all would lecture.

"How come my dad is out there then?" I said as I thumbed toward never-never land.

"You learn this part of the game, son, and you'll beat them someday."

"Thanks, mister." I'd say as I thought "*Now get lost.*"

Every yahoo, with or without knickers, had some opinion on "how to" and each instruction would contradict the previous one.

"Keep your head down",

"Put your weight on your left foot",

"No, your right foot",

"Lean forward",

"Lean back."

"I'm getting a headache so I'm going to sit in the shade."

"Drink some water."

"Yeah, thanks." And I thought again *"Now get lost."*

I really did have a headache so I went and sat in the shade with some water until Passover. I am Catholic so my version of Passover was waiting until the plague of advice-toads passed by. I would have killed a lamb and put blood on my putter if it would have kept them away.

Yogi Berra, a philosophical hero of mine, once said, "You can notice a lot just by watching." So I'd watch people. It was funny how the little things rule your life. They would each take out three balls because that's how many balls are in a new sleeve. They would drop them on the practice green, putt those three balls and have a conversation that neither one listened to.

"It's too fast."

"It's too slow."

"I made two out of three."

"This place sucks!"

"Ready?"

"Ready."

Apparently, this was the entire warm up one needed before heading out.

People were coming off the eighteenth green every ten minutes. I started to see groups who left after my dad coming up the eighteenth.

"Oh yeah, we saw them. They were nice enough to let us play through."

"Nice Enough? Play through?" I think I am getting to understand my Mom's lesson on this left-handed compliment thing.

When I got old enough I would get to join them. The years did not make them any better. I guess because they did not know "where the game was really played." We certainly didn't practice. They'd give me a sleeve of balls, I'd pour them out on the green and I'd putt them.

"Ready?"

"Ready." I said having the lingo down pretty good by now.

Eventually Dad gave me my own bag and some clubs so I could slow up the pace of play with them. The Irish starter could not find an English guy to put with us, so we were a threesome. We were still slow. Losing a ball on every hole will do that.

We always had someone on our ass. My father would be philosophic, "There is nothing slower than the group in front of you or faster than the pain in the ass behind you."

If you listened carefully you could hear guns cocking a few groups back. So this is golf! I'd still rather be playing baseball. We'd stop for lunch as the starter always reminded us how good the egg salad was and to avoid the pizza.

** Ah, that explains a lot. **

Lofty Expectations

For a few years when our ages aligned like planets, my dad, my two brothers and I enjoyed a game or two as a foursome. My brother, Billy, was only 13 and had not paid his dues on the practice green but Dad felt he was ready. My herculean brother, Bobby, had cut down on the weights, lost a few ripples and gained the semblance of a golf swing. I think it was then that he started to gain Jack's nightmare, *Great Expectations*.

The reality of breaking 100 was within his sight as we approached the 16th hole. He reviewed his scorecard as he calculated, *"All I need is a bogey on each hole and the crowd would cheer as I came off the 18th."* Oh we could read his every thought like an open book with two pages. To us breaking 100 was like pitching a perfect game; naturally we kept quiet about the possibility.

It was not to be. I apologize, I did not want to spoil it for you but Jack insisted that I tell you before you got any lofty expectations of your own. You see having lofty expectations for other people is not allowed either, according to Jack.

The 16th was downhill with nothing in the front to get in your way. The green was flat. It was a *simple* 150 yard par three. *Simple* except that the green was hanging in mid-air. To the left was a gigantic cliff, *thousands of miles down*, as was the back and right of the green. At least this is the way it must have looked to my brother. A slim peninsula of hope surrounded by valleys of death! A *simple* downhill 130 yard shot down the middle would roll up perfectly; that was all that was needed. Bobby led off and after his ninth practice swing he stepped up to the ball.

"Hmmm", I thought, *"He forgot one."*

Sure enough, hoping to hit it before the devil could catch him he pull-hooked it slightly left of the green. He leaned to the right to help bring the ball back on path. The ball had problems of its own and ignored its owner's body English. Lee Trevino put it perfectly, "You can talk to a fade but a hook won't listen."

Bobby said absolutely nothing. He pointed at the green with his club and walked backwards not to lose sight of the flag as he reached back for his hand cart. It was a staring contest between the flag and my brother. I actually thought I saw the flag shaking; I mean there wasn't any wind. It really was a good shot; it was just a little left of target. The rest of us sculled our balls up on to the green for possible birdies because well, because golf has its own unique reward system. We headed toward the green in silence.

Bobby walked his hand cart to what was really only 30 feet down. He could not see the flag so I held it up in the air. My arm was aching as I awaited all 10 practice swings and then it happened. His ball came up like magic right at the flag. It bounced once, twice and then rolled off the other side about thirty feet down.

"Aw!" Dad was sympathetic.

"It was good but it rolled off." I added.

"You can probably use the same club though." as Billy found a positive.

Bobby appeared and his head bobbed up and down as he marched uphill to our level. He left his handcart in front of the green pointing the grip of his wedge at the flag like a matador. Another hoist of the flag, 10 practice swings and up toward the flag again and off the other side.

After playing volleyball with the green four times my brother disappeared for another attempt. Each attempt seemed closer until the fate of over-compensation took its place; his shot came up short rolled back to his feet? Bobby did not say a single word. If it were me, truck drivers on close by I-91 would swerve out of control from my language. Bobby said not a word.

His next shot nearly made it to the green but rolled all the way back downhill to his feet again. Then we heard a helicopter go by. Actually it was a wedge acting like a helicopter. It was a well-conceived toss as it went in the direction of the next tee.

** If you are going to lose your temper make sure it is directed at the next hole. **

"Thanks Jack."

** You're welcome. **

I cannot explain how uncharacteristic this is for my brother. He is not one to lose control. He shows no anger. It was rare that he uttered a discouraging word and his skies were not cloudy but for this one day. It was this day that golf would tear the inner beast from within him. It dangled the carrot of success before him and then, it would yank it away!

Bobby ceased control. He went over retrieved his whirly-bird and said quite matter-of-factly, "I'll see you guys on the next tee."

He jerked the cart so hard the handle came out of the holder. He raised the handle like an executioner but then he lowered it slowly. He shoved the handle in hard, pointed a finger at it (index finger in case you got carried away) and marched toward the next tee. The wounded handcart could barely keep up with him.

Dad, Billy and I made birdies but we did not tell Bobby.

"Boy, I can't wait to tell Bobby. I got my first birdie." Billy said.

"Good idea," I agreed, "and then you can ask him what he got on that hole."

"Not if either of you wants to live." Dad said.

So due to our kind consideration and, of course, the chance of physical harm we took Dad's advice. We gave Bobby a 9 on that hole. He may have done better but he insisted on our family maximum. After relinquishing his high hopes, Bobby calmed down. He had given up the dream and because he did, he made par on the next two holes. He shot 102 for the day. He was good at math but he kept checking his numbers over and over again. I shot 108 and was happy to do so. Out of the woods you could hear Jack whisper.

** You know, things could be a lot worse, you'll see. **

Enjoy Your Lunch

My dad's boss, Sean Fitzpatrick, came up to New England to see us for a few days. He belonged to a country club and had been playing and practicing for years. I got to see what real good golf mixed with expectations looked like. What is that about? I'll tell you. It is a cocktail, mixed with ice cubes frozen over by cold-hearted self-assurance. It is about a perfect swing stirred with reckless abandon and a thick wallet to back it up.

Mr. Fitzpatrick was a big strong guy. He was Irish and looked like Brian Keith but bigger. He could hit the ball 300 yards even with 1960's equipment. He did however; violate all of the principles that Jack had so carefully laid out. His expectations were way too high.

He was a big boss at his office and everyone and everything would be required to do exactly what he told them. The course was no exception; it was just another office employee to him. He had very specific instructions on where his golf ball should and should not go. Sometimes he would even announce his plans and called his shots like a pool player running the table.

"I think I'll take this three-iron and draw it around that tree to the green. That will give me a chance for an eagle. I've got a good chance of breaking par today."

** *Lofty, lofty, lofty…nay, nay, nay!* **

The ball took off as stated and drew according to precise instruction but when it hit the ground something made it jump to the left; a hard left. The ball apparently had made other plans. It was tired of having the crap knocked out of it; so it scurried deep into the woods like a prison break.

"Damn it!" Snap was all we heard as he broke the club in half like a toothpick in his bare hands.

You see he did not listen to our friend Jack and his three-iron paid the price. He would finish the round with somewhere close to nine of his fourteen clubs and still managed a 73. He was not happy. Talk about lofty goals!?!

As I got older I still only played with my dad once a year. By then I could drink and we would laugh and share beers, dirty jokes and horrible golf. We would let people play through and never break 100 but we would break for lunch.

"Did you bring the scorecard?" Dad would ask.

"No", having learned from my brother, "I left it in the cart."

"Good. At least we can enjoy our lunch."

But Jack Knows You

Then we'd order our egg salad on rye and a few beers. My dad still had that one goal; he wanted to break 100. He got close a few times but time was not on his

23

side. He passed away too early. He never got to break 100. I loved my dad. Oddly enough I was beginning to like New England, too, but I drew the line with the Red Sox. Dad never got to see his beloved team win and I hated them for that. When they finally did win I hoped that somehow my dad got to see it.

After Dad had passed away I went back to the faith and gave up golf. I played baseball; far too much baseball. After two very nice knee surgeries, 45 stitches, a tilted spine and my 33rd birthday I gave up third base and hardball for good. Jack could not have been happier. You can tell because he hardly ever stopped by after that.

I played softball for a few years but it lacked the stitching. I needed to challenge myself so I dusted off the old clubs my dad had given me.

I love sports but I don't like watching them. I never sat well on the bench and the bench never sat well with me. I'm going to be good at this if it kills me! I was nearly 40 when I took the game up seriously; too seriously.

Because of a subtle hint or two, my wife bought me a new set of clubs, a bag and some spikes. I no sooner opened the gifts when the phone rang. It was Jack. I don't know how he knew. Jack always knows.

** Congratulations, now you're an asshole. **

2: Sweet Revenge

Forget the Bad Ones

"Golf is the perfect thing to do on Sunday because you spend more time praying than you would in church."
- *Unknown*

My wife had started taking up the game. She took lessons because, unlike most of us, she has a brain which she actually uses. I wonder how much lower my handicap would be if I only put a little thought into what I was doing. Once I get to the course I forget all of that crap and try to make impossible shots that are not in my bag of tricks. My wife visualizes each shot before she hits it. I'm not sure but I think this might violate a Jack principle. Anyway, who has time for that? I remember the first time she was ready for the course. It seems every state has a Brentwood Country Club so we decided one morning to give ours the true blessing of our company.

"This nice couple is going to join you." the starter said to the twosome. The starter is a god at any public course and his words are the law and are not to be questioned.

"Oh, that's nice" one said.

The other guy followed with, "Yeah, great." Making two positives sound negative.

"I'm Wayne and this is my wife Stephanie."

"I'm Bill and this is my friend Greg."

Both men were in their 60s and their equipment showed a lot of miles. It was obvious that the two had a regular game and they looked concerned.

"Don't worry we won't hold you up. My wife's had lessons. She's pretty good."

"I went for lessons once and the guy totally screwed me up." The back of his bag said Greg Schmidt, Chiropractor.

"How ironic is that?" I said.

** *Good one.* ** No one caught that but Jack.

Greg turned, stepped ahead of Bill and me and teed his ball up. You can learn more about a guy in one day on the golf course than you can in a year in an office. This guy is rude and he believes that his time is more important than the rest of us. There was no practice swing. He was really in some kind of hurry.

** *He probably has an appointment to cripple someone this afternoon.* **

I could hear Jack snicker. People think I am nuts because I burst into laughter but it is not me it's Jack. I swear. Anyway, Greg caught the ball with the bottom stripe of the club head. It never left the ground more than 6 inches and barely made the fairway about 50 yards away.

"Thank God you passed the ladies tee!" Bill laughed.

I was still recovering from Jack's comment when Stephanie elbowed me. "Control yourself."

Bill Miller was in great shape. He had said he ran a local gym and smoked a good drive down the middle. I followed but not as far. As we drove up to the ladies' tee Greg was thankfully quiet.

Stephanie has curly blonde hair that people pay good money to copy at the beauty parlor. She had a pink hat with a blue brim that shades two huge blue-green eyes and a big white smile. She's five foot two in her spikes, and a little over a hundred pounds. She has white shorts and two white spikes size 3½ but she can't see anything below her yellow golf shirt because there are these two big things in the way.

*** Oh. Nice out on that one. ***

"Shut up Jack."

*** Hey, it's what I do. ***

She's eleven years younger than me and ten years smarter than Jack and, be forewarned; she is one-hundred percent Long Island girl.

"I'm so nervous I can't stop my hands from shaking." This is coming from a woman who has jumped from planes and dove with sharks.

"Relax, Honey."

She walked up to the red markers, put the ball on the tee and tossed the head cover to the side. She took one practice swing, stepped up to the ball and cracked the ball high and long. The ball waved to the poor little chiropractor's ball, landed by mine on a fly and came to rest next to Bill's lengthy tee shot.

"Holy shit!" Not sure who said it. It was just a reaction. "Sorry Ma'am! But that was some drive!" It was the guy from the gym and he was impressed.

"Thanks, Bill." Stephanie said as she put the head cover on with the biggest smile since Alice in Wonderland.

My wife had found a teaching pro near where she worked. She went a couple of days a week and we would go to the driving range. I could tell she was ready to play; certainly more ready than most.

No one was more surprised than Stephanie. The first time on a real course can be scary and this one started with a long par 5. She struggled a bit with the irons; she chipped well but three putted. She lost the big smile as she got back in the cart.

"What's the matter, sweetheart?"

"I got a ten on that hole." Her lower lip was quivering and I thought she might even cry. She was so disappointed that I could not stand it.

"Honey, one thing about golf is that you have to remember your good shots. Forget the bad ones like they never happened."

She thought for a moment and looked at her fingers. That big smile returned to her face as she beamed, "Okay, I got a 6 then!"

You Can't Even Drive a Golf Cart

After a few holes of looking for the bone-cracker's lost balls the group behind us was on our tail. We were still on the group in front of us so there was no point in letting them play through. After about three holes of impatience a ball came bouncing up between my wife and me. I stood out of the cart and gave them a "what's up with that" look; I had my palms in the air as my arms extended outward. They waved with, what I felt was, a mild apology.

It was only two holes later, my wife had gotten back in the cart when we were heading for the green and another ball came bouncing past us. I have a temper and I was going to let them see it! Without any warning I cut the wheel left to turn around and give these guys a real "what for".

A loud but fading, "Whoa, whoa, whoa…" was all that I heard as I looked over to the empty seat where once sat my dear wife. I looked back to see alternating colors of pink and yellow clothing tumbling like those you might see in a clothes dryer.

"Oops", I had just dumped my wife assholes and elbows out of the cart. Great! This is going to take the sting out of giving hell to those guys. Now I have to go back and retrieve my wife first.

** Nice. At least you have your priorities. **

"Are you all right, honey?"

"What the hell are you doing!?"

"I was going to confront those bastards."

I heard the wheels of two carts coming.

"Gees, is she okay? Sorry about the ball again. Are you okay, Miss?"

"Yeah, I'll be fine; I'd be better if I was driving!"

Some nervous laughter followed as we put little miss grass-stains back in the cart.

"Are you sure you're okay, Miss?"

"Yes, thanks guys." said my little trooper.

My temper had completely fizzled because I endangered my wife far worse than a rolling golf ball. I tried to muster up some form of dignity.

"We'd let you play through but there's no place to go."

"We know. Sorry, that won't happen again."

"Okay, thanks guys. See you later."

As we drove off I heard "Jerk." but it was not from behind me, and it wasn't Jack; it was much closer than that.

Revenge is a Dish

I think I was still rattled when I got to the next tee box. I hit my shot deep into the woods on the right. We spent about five minutes looking for *my* ball this time. We found it. It took us a while to finish the hole but the guys behind us waited until we were on the green. It was the easiest par four on the course and I took a six. Greg could not wait to announce that he had beaten me with a five but his wind was knocked out of him in a hurry.

"So did I." Stephanie declared.

"I made par." Bill smiled.

We made our way to the next tee box. Even though we took a while on that hole we still had to wait again. It was a par three and there was a group not yet on the green. Another group was teeing off at the next hole.

"This place puts too many people on the course for the pace of play." Bill calculated.

"Yeah, it would be faster if they played better and did not have to look for lost balls." Greg was beginning to manipulate my bones with his words. I was thinking about how I'd like to adjust his nose.

"Seems to me that you lost two balls on the front nine; didn't you, Greg?" Bill whipped him like the proverbial rented mule as he gave me and Steph a wink.

"Yeah, well I didn't hold anyone up."

We finally teed up after what felt like 20 minutes. Bill hit a great shot but it rolled off the back and Greg hit his first green in regulation of the day.

"Nice shot." Steph was the first to say.

Bill said, "About time! Hey, only kidding buddy, great shot."

Although I hated to say anything of kindness to this moron, I felt compelled by etiquette. "Good shot."

I hit mine on the green inside of Greg's as Steph and Bill clapped and Greg made what sounded like an intestinal noise. Maybe it was a compliment or maybe it was just gas. Steph wasted no time as she marched up to the red tees and hit her shot to the left by the cart path. She chips pretty well so she would still have a good shot at par. She was still brushing off the grass stains as we got out of the cart. I was taking out my putter and shedding the head cover.

"I'll take my wedge and my putter." as she lifted the wedge from her bag with one hand under the other.

She repeated the one-hand-under-the-other one time too many as she lost the end of the wedge; the club head started to fall.

Whack, I actually heard the sound inside my head moments before the pain set in. I thought I got hit with a golf ball.

"Oh God, sorry, honey." I heard her say as I realized it was not a ball at all. My wife had just clobbered me.

The head is a weird part of the body when it comes to blows. It exaggerates everything.

*** And so do you. ***

This was not a penny falling from the Empire State Building; this was a fallen club head and gravity from less than three feet. I removed my hat as a lump started to form and blood started trickling down my face. It is not like I am not used to similar injuries. I had been on the wrong end of a few fists in my time along with a few errant bounces at third base. Bill brought over a few napkins and Greg rushed over with his lack of medical skills.

"Here hold this against it until we get some ice." Bill said.

Greg said, "I see the cart girl over there I'll get some ice." as if it was his idea first.

"Thanks, I'll be fine." I said.

"Oh honey, let me see it. I'm so sorry, sweetheart."

The napkins helped but they were sticky. I found a handkerchief in my bag, wrapped the ice that Greg got for me and put my hat back on to keep the pressure. It was more from the bump that tore my scalp so when the swelling went down, it pretty much stopped.

I'll be fine" I repeated. "Thanks for the ice and stuff."

"Do you want to stop and go in?" Steph suggested.

"No honey. It will stop and I'll be fine."

"Okay but let me know."

We walked up to the green as Steph prepared her chip shot. She was obviously still quite shaken as she almost chipped in for birdie.

Hell Hath No Fury

We all made pars as the cart girl drove up. I got some more ice and a few cold beers to bring the swelling down from the inside; a proven Irish medicinal technique.

"Seems fair to me." Bill seemed philosophical.

"What's that?" I asked.

"Well, you dump her out the cart and then she clobbers you."

"Hey, I did not do that on purpose." Steph complained.

"Hell hath no fury..." Bill laughed as did we all.

I wasn't really playing great but not bad either. I looked down at the scorecard. I knew Steph had been doing well, especially on the back. She looked over my shoulder.

"I'm beating you." She smiled.

"Yeah, in more ways than one." I laughed.

"Yeah, "in more ways than one" is right. If you drove better, I wouldn't beat you." was her quick retort.

I chewed on that for a while as I rubbed my head and then I heard someone snickering off in the distance.

"Ah yes, hell hath no fury, indeed."

3: Got to Have a Game

My friend Bob once said to me that you've got to have a game. I did not understand him right off. "You mean *my* game?"

"No, no. What I mean is you've got to have a regular game. You know; a group of guys that you can count on to be there on a regular basis. If you don't have a regular game you have inconsistency, if you don't have a regular game you don't practice, and you will always be scrambling to find 'a game' and you will not get any better."

Bob is right of course but there a lot of games out there that are not 'regular'.

Men's Clubs and Characters

You take a lot of things for granted in life. If you belong to a *good* men's club you have found a unique treasure. You can always spot a good men's club; from the outside, it may have a waiting list or require a recommendation from a member or two. From the inside it has rules, it has tournaments, it has set tee times but mostly it has camaraderie. People who like being together so much that they see each other more than just once a week. They have golf trips, hang out after for a few drinks and often see each other off the course. If you don't have a club like this all you have is a few tee times and some guys who have little else.

Before I moved to Florida I played with our men's club on Long Island. I did not realize what I had and it took me a while to find another. I still travel and I go back to Long Island every summer. But no matter how good or how bad your club is, it will always have its *characters*. And like they say; if you look around and you don't see any, then it is probably you.

The Chosen Few

We met at 5:30 AM every Saturday morning at the club where the foursomes were arranged. It is pot luck; at least I used to think so. As you go through a year of Saturdays you meet different players; some you like, some you can tolerate and then, there are those "others". These *undesirables* have no defined shape or size, it is more within their demeanor; it is part of their self-involved being. Get your highlighters ready because I promise to hit them all, the cheats, the bad company and those that are so slow that they may have not even come in yet.

Some clubs let the same foursomes stick together every week. If you run the club and you lack energy and enthusiasm this is a homerun; you just copy last week's sheet, put a new date on the top and collect the money. But they say familiarity breeds contempt; well, it breeds more than that. You put the same four primates together and the alpha ape will run that pack. Out in the golf jungle, he/she will 'interpret' the club rules and which ones apply to his/her given situation. This is the formula for corruption which we've grown to accept from Washington, but there is no room for this kind of behavior on the golf course.

You have to mix it up now and again. You can call it checks and balances or call it getting to know the other members. Pot luck is not totally pot luck if members chose who they would and would not play with. If that field of whom you will play with narrows down to only three people; this is a red flag.

*** Yeah; you're either a cheater or someone's bitch. ***

Your Turn in the Barrel

Everyone knows that I will pretty much play with anyone.

"Wayne will play with anyone."

"He's a nice guy." Some would say.

"He's an idiot." is more often the vote.

A lot of guys had nicknames often chosen by our presidents Don and Ted. Don runs the Thursday group. He is a dead ringer for Gary Player; the same height and build and even has a practice swing exactly like him. The swing he uses on the actual shot, however, is totally different. He runs the club with a firm hand as it should be. Don's personality is a bit rough around the edges especially when he meets a new member.

"I've heard about you. Funny, you don't even look gay."

Ted runs the Saturday league. He has a rounder face, a bit grayer, a bit taller, and a bit stockier than Don. He loves to tell you the latest joke on the front nine and one on the back nine. It's the same joke. You can tell him your joke and then later he will come back and tell it to you.

"Did you hear the one about the priest and the rabbi?"

"I just told you that joke."

"Well it goes like this…."

You might as well sit back and listen. He'll probably tell it better than you did anyway. He used to run a mechanic shop and ran a tight ship at the men's club. Here's a common conversation with Ted or Don to a member's complaint.

"I'm not playing with him!"

"Yeah, well you are today."

"I'm leaving."

"Good, don't come back."

"Oh, alright fine, but just this once."

There are nicknames which are not necessarily bad; they are based on incidences or character traits. If they like you your nickname is something like, shadow, biz-buzz, weasel or the phantom; these were standard form.

"Hey Biz, who're you playing with today?"

"I'm with Larry, Ralph and biz-biz-buz-biz." His answer starts out loud enough but trails off to an inaudible end.

"Oh, that's nice."

"Biz-biz-buz-biz."

"Yeah, you too."

"Hey, has anyone seen Phantom?"

"He was out on the putting green with the Weasel but then when I went to get him…well, I'm not really sure."

These were good guys with defining traits. If you were one of the *undesirables*, however, you got a less dignified name tag. An *undesirable* is someone you do not want to play with and, like any other club, we have our share.

First and foremost were the Pig and the Putts, or Putz if you prefer. Another *fun* but harmless guy was the Parrot. "Both of the three of them" as Yogi Berra would say, were paired together almost every Saturday.

"Hey Parrot, good morning."

"Good morning, good morning to you too."

Usually the three P's in the pod went out as a threesome unless some poor bastard was new and yet unpunished. If the amount of players was evenly divisible by four, someone had to take his turn in the barrel. I used to have this recurring nightmare that I died and went to hell. I'd have a seat right next to my friend Jack.

** You should be so lucky. **

Anyway, during this bedtime-sweating-sheet-turner, I'd get the old "good news, bad news" from the Prince of Darkness, himself.

"You are going to play golf every day." said Satan. "Your foursome will be "The Putz, the Parrot, The Piggy and YOU! Ah, hah, ah, hah, hah…."

I'd wake up in a cold shivering sweat unable to unwrap myself from the sheets. My pillow was drenched and crunched up like a little ball. I must have strangled it during the night. It was only a dream thank God.

Many weeks had gone by and I had forgotten all about that dream. But on this one awful Saturday, *a day that will ring out in infamy*, by all that is unholy in this world, it happened. This was certainly not what my friend Bob had in mind when he said, "You've got to have a game." This is golf's answer to waterboarding. I had woken up on what would have been a *beautiful* Saturday at oh-dark-thirty.

As is the tradition, each Saturday they would figure out the foursomes at about 6:00 in the morning. This meant I needed to be up before 5:00 AM. I am NOT a morning person. My wife is. I'd rather hug my normally dry pillow for a few more hours. But I made it to the club in time for "The Clubhouse Special", which is a ham and egg with American cheese on a poppy-seeded Kaiser roll and a cup of coffee. Usually someone orders one from April before me so I just point. She hates when I do that but it's too early. Some parts of me wake up faster than others and my mouth is still asleep. Charlie is the chef and he makes the best breakfast on earth. The smells of crisping bacon are drifting in waves from the kitchen.

"Make that bacon instead of ham will you." Ted said.

"Do you want to point all over again or do you still want the ham?" April asked.

"Ham, please." Damn! I could have pointed and had the bacon.

"Okay." She heads to the kitchen pleased with herself for forcing me to talk.

While you wait for *The Special* you sip your coffee, pay your fees and get the news on who's got who. Or is it whom? I squeezed the money out of my wallet as the two pawns of Satan show me my foursome. My worst nightmare!

"You're kidding, right!?"

"Nope, it just worked out that way. Oh and by the way, your group is last up."

"That's real nice. Thank you, thank you so very much." And I gave him half of a peace sign.

"Hey, no problem."

As I walked away my cell phone rang. It was Jack.

** S*o how's it going? Ah, hah, ah, hah, hah....* ** and he simply hung up.

"Bastard!" I cried out and shook my head wondering how on earth Jack always knows what he knows. So now it's a matter of waiting.

The *Wading* Game

I think the worst part of being on death row is the waiting. It would sure be better to go first and get this over with. The men's club had about 12 foursomes that day. Figuring about 8 minutes between tee times, eleven groups in front of me, that's a good 88 minutes. It never goes by as quickly as the math. I should have taken a nap but I was afraid I might have another nightmare worse than this reality. I waded while I waited. I waded through the crowded putting green. Then I chipped while the Parrot chirped. I putted while the Putz close talked me. I waved him away and excused myself to the bathroom or anywhere so I did not have to spend more time at this then I had to. I decided to pick up a few survival items at the bar. May made me a double Bloody Mary to beat the band.

"I heard the news and I think you are going to need this." May said. "And if I were you I'd take a six pack to go and then reload at the turn." May laughed.

"Thanks, May. I'll need it."

I went back to the practice green. I was thinking that since Artie and I are out-of-towners we were given these nice choice tees times; last and second to last. As Artie and I exchanged a few "swing easy, good luck" comments I noticed my foursome was incomplete.

"Where's Piggy?" I shouted impatiently.

Artie said, "He had to drop a few kids off in the pool."

"Yeah, he had to take a dump, you know, a dump!" The Parrot mocked.

*** Ha ha ha ah ha hah. ***

They even got Jack on that one. Normally I would have joined in the laughter but we were on deck and NOW he decides to hit the head!!? Now I'm brick red. Artie took off after his perfect drive and full head of dark hair with his pleasantly chosen foursome. Obviously somebody loves Artie; God decided to take all of my hair and grant me this special foursome in return. Where is Piggy?

"Two hours waiting for our turn and he waits until now to take a shit!!?" as I open my hands to the heavens.

"Oh, good idea', said the Putz, "I'll be right back."

Great, now two of them are gone! We haven't even teed up yet and I'm already hemorrhaging. I had already asked the three stooges on the putting green if they were walking or driving. They all said that they were walking so I rented a cart. This is a must if you are playing with J.J. Putz. If you walk the course with the Putz, he will close talk you between shots or in your backswing or while you're taking a leak in the woods. You also have to have a cart so you can find their shots. They will have no idea where their ball went.

But most importantly you need a cart for some 'alone time', a chance to get some air and calm down before you kill one of them and become the hot topic on the evening news. I can almost see the Suffolk Police chasing my golf cart down Sunrise highway as I try to escape. Helicopters would cover the whole pathetic scene from the air.

** Maybe you should buy a glove at the pro shop that "doesn't fit"? **

With or without the quorum of our foursome it is "ready-golf" and we are up. I'm more than ready to hit. Having a good solid case of the red-ass I blistered a drive down the left side where it nestles against the tree, the only damned tree, on the entire first hole.

I spin around but there is really no one to blame but myself. I should have gone home with some painful excuse; a toothache, a hang nail, I have to go to New Hampshire, anything, anything but this.

The Piggy

Piggy finally surfaced from the bathroom door of the club. Red 'Piggy' Pika is an odd hare to say the least. With all his idiosyncrasies you just have to have a guy like this in your club. If your club is short on characters, we'll send you one of ours.

3: Got to Have a Game

He is wearing what once was a beautiful short sleeved plaid dress shirt. Anyway it met the club's "collar requirement." Not to worry though, he will be shedding this to expose an even older tee shirt as soon as he is out of sight of the club house. According to his weight he should be six-three but he is only five-seven. He is a furry little animal in plaid shorts to compliment that differently-plaided shirt. His two black socks are half-way up his calves and at the bottom of this picture is some kind of footwear made from dead animal skins. Not too many people can carry this outfit off; but somehow it all fits him.

Red is more or less a stand-up guy. He plays the ball down and he never cheats, at lease in his mind. As a matter of fact he may miss an easy putt or two or even add a stroke when it doesn't matter. You see he has what Don calls a *well-managed* handicap. He is a 36. Yet, he plays ready golf and will not slow you down unless you're bothering his space. Piggy tees it up but there is someone standing on the tee box. It is me. I am well behind him but somehow he knows; maybe he smells soap.

"Do you mind?" As he waves me away with his hand above his ass like he just cut one.

This high handicapper cracks one down the middle about two-hundred yards.

"This cannot be happening to me!!" as I atheistically give up all hope and kick my cart. "Whose form of justice is this that I have to give this fuzzy little Bilbo Baggins 28 strokes!!?"

"Where's J.J.?" I shouted in anger. "He was with you!"

"Here he comes. Here he comes now." The Parrot repeats.

** You can either be the one everyone wants to hang with or the one everyone wants to hang. **

The Putz

Mr. J.J. Putts is a bit taller than Piggy and he is now heading toward the tee in a hurry. I looked over his shoulder to see the janitor on all fours. Apparently he wasn't feeling too well. Never follow the wrong person to the bathroom.

** We'll call that Rule number 2, then. **

"I thought you were going to the bathroom?"

"Maybe later." J.J. said.

No matter J.J. would pee at every hole anyway. He is a bit graying these days; he is clean shaven and conservatively dressed wearing something that was fashionable during Truman's presidency. He walks around the tee box picking up every broken tee and tossing it anywhere out of his sight at times hitting a fellow competitor. No matter, you do not even exist in his world. This is his way of clearing the tee box. All of the unbroken tees are now in his pocket. He is ready to go through his routine.

The Putz tees the ball and walks behind it for the line. Looking down the fairway he drags his club Art Carney style and addresses the ball. After what seems to be enough time to fire off a few Hail Mary's he steps away unsure of the line he just took. He repeats the process and looks at me because I am within 25 feet of him and he can see my shoes, I guess. I got in my cart as he restarts his painful procedure.

I reflect for a moment. "I am going to kill him today and no one will convict me. I know you are there Jack; snickering off a few, "I told you so's."

** Okay. I was going to wait until later but now is good. **

The Putz swings back and forth in a fluid motion but some cruel lack of talent causes him to skull the ball about 100 yards.

"Well your alignment worked. It's down the middle. Right down the middle!" the Parrot announces.

Putz mutters something and grabs his pull cart behind him. The Parrot follows. J.J. Putz is talking to the Parrot about six inches from the Parrot's face as they walk. The Parrot tries to walk around him but J.J. is all over him like a point guard. The Parrot walked straight and J.J. was striding him sideways; they looked like a lobster and a crab vying over the same piece of dead fish.

"Aren't *you* going to hit?" I asked the Parrot.

"Oh, yeah, oh yeah, sure." The Parrot turns and walks back to the tee box.

The Putz walks to the side more for protection than for any courtesy. I haven't moved my cart yet. I haven't moved my cart in almost an hour. The foursome behind us wants to know if they can play through.

I give them a questioning shrug with two palms up as I point out, "It's the first hole, for Christ's sake!!"

And The Parrot

The Parrot is well dressed and in fashion. He is undoubtedly the shortest and the most-likable of the group. He is neither fat nor skinny. He is virtually harmless. His round smiling face frames almost baby-like features for a man in his seventies; he looks far younger than his years. He causes the people around him to age more quickly. He's the Dorian Gray of the club and we are his picture in the attic. All of his fine features become unglued by a pair of lips that form a beak that is in a constant motion.

He would be perfect as one of those characters you see in the Twilight Zone. You can almost hear Rod Serling, "Mr. E. Jeffrey Parrot is a quiet well-mannered gentle man, living in a quiet well-mannered gentle house. You see, Mr. Parrot's wife never lets him speak at home. Now he finds himself in a place where he can talk without stopping, right here at the Twilight Zone country club."

They do not call him the Parrot because he repeats what others say; they call him the Parrot because he repeats what 'he' says.

The Parrot wastes no time on the tee box. He tees his ball, steps back and swings like the Venus de Milo but with arms. I do not mean it is a thing of beauty. His swing has no body movement. His hips and shoulders are motionless eliminating any type of power as his arms seem to fly off his body.

Crack! He hits it square on the club face and airs the ball about 80 yards with another 15 yards of roll. Pathetically he has not reached the skulled ball of the Putz.

The Parrot smiles, "I nailed that one. Boy, I nailed that one."

"You might hit it further if you turned your shoulders." Putz provides some unsolicited advice.

"I might hurt something" said the Parrot. "What if I hurt something?" he disguises his repetition as a question.

"You mean like your score for instance?" I added my own two-cents.

The Parrot laughed, at what, he does not know but he laughed because everyone else did. The Parrot is my partner as we play against J.J. Putz and his oddly manicured partner.

It's Only a Game

Golf courses are lined with trees, grass and all the beauty that nature can provide. This particular course runs along the Great South Bay and peaks out at a hole we call Gibraltar. Deer run around as if you are not there and rabbits drop calling cards in the line of your putt. Swans swim in the ponds and give you notice when you are near their young. The wildlife does not know enough to rake their footprints in the traps and this includes players of equal intelligence. Whatever cards life deals you or whatever foursome golf gives you, you must play this game to the end. I would enjoy the day, play the game and take whatever this day would deliver mainly because this course has a special gift; an endless supply of alcohol.

We call the game "Two-and-One" which is basically a two dollar Nassau and a dollar for each bippy[1]. The Nassau bet gets its name from the Nassau Country Club on Long Island, where the format was invented in the early 1900s by club captain John B. Coles Tappan. Our Nassau has automatic two-down presses. So if you are two holes down and lose the next hole you're 3-1, that is, 3 down on the original bet and 1 down on the press. If

---

[1] A bippy, sometimes called "the junk", is a natural birdie; a chippie from off the green or an up and down from the bunker called a sandy. Chippies and sandies only count if they are for par or better. Closest to the pin on a par 3 or after the 3rd shot on a par 5 are also bippies. I know; it's complicated.

you have a really bad day you could lose about $20 tops. Usually it ends up around 6 or 7 dollars so it's not about the money. Well, okay, for a cheap bastard like me it is, but not for most of the guys.

Piggy is heading down the rough along the water to scrounge for golf balls as J.J. tries to bum a ride on my cart.

"Get out." I said.

"Oh yeah, right. I should not do that so close to the clubhouse."

"Yeah that and I don't want you in my cart."

I did not like spending the extra money for a cart but I got it to stay away from this pain in the ass. No way would I let him jump in especially for free. I had loaded myself up with my well spiked Bloody Mary to start the day and a six pack of Bud for medicinal purposes. This would hold me until the turn. The starter agreed that I was going to need it and he gave me the sign of the cross before he waved goodbye.

I did not like spending the extra money for their beer either. The guy who runs the food and beverage has not yet seen the ghost of Christmas Past. He charges $5 for a domestic beer which is about $2 more than other courses.

*** He's not the one forcing you to drink, is he? ***

I gave Jack the finger, finished the Bloody in one hand and popped a beer in defiance with the other as I drove down the first fairway using my right knee to steer. I got out pitched my ball to the fairway from behind that lone freakin' tree and got back in the cart with my club. I was going to use it again anyway. I slammed down the rest of the first beer. Eventually the *happy few* all met on the first green but not before Putz found the bunker.

"Footprint!" He declared.

Our club rules allow you to smooth and place the ball if you are in a footprint in a bunker. It's a good rule because almost no one rakes a bunker here.

"Wait a minute Putz, let me see." I said because of my faith in him. I walked over to check it out. "That's a deer foot print!"

"Doesn't matter" he said "rules are rules."

"Fine" I conceded. I had another 8 holes to go before the turn and I only had 5 beers left. Anyway, it does not matter; the Putz couldn't get out of a bunker with a backhoe.

J.J. Putz raked and smoothed the entire trap because he thought about putting it. He realized he needed a shovel to flatten the lip, so he opted for his sand wedge. Then he made a little peak of sand and placed his ball on top. It was still a downhill lie. He scrapes his sand wedge along the sand to get it out of the way on his backswing then miraculously hits the ball onto the green.

"That's a penalty. You can't improve your lie by scraping the sand away on your back swing."

The Parrot agreed by repeating me and then himself.

"That's a penalty, that's a penalty."

Putz slams his club into the bunker and stomps across the entire trap without raking it. He three-puts the green as usual and storms off the green to his golf bag.

"Let's see; on in three plus two for the penalty and three putts, hmmm…eight Putz?" I could not resist.

"Yes, whatever… damn it!" He agrees as he heads to the woods to start marking his territory.

Since gentleman J.J. Putz went out of turn we all finished the hole. Our 36 handicap made par after lipping out a 25 foot birdie attempt. Parrot made six and I somehow scratched out a bogey. I had to punch out from behind "The Only Tree", hit my third to the green and then two putted. I really did not expect much this day so I got in the cart and pounded down another $5 Bud. I broke the pencil writing down the scores but the starter had given me three more.

"Here, you're going to need these too." He had said as I left.

We got to this par three. The Piggy was short in a bunker which he could not get out of and said he had a six to ensure his handicap.

"Five right?" I corrected him.

"Oh yeah, five." He agreed.

Piggy Pika doesn't think padding is cheating. He dresses poorly and consoles himself that he is not good with big numbers. The Parrot had taken his driver out and got the greenie and he sunk his first birdie putt since

1949. Mr. Putz also hit the green with his tee shot. He took a four on the hole because of his flat-stick prowess. I missed the green but got up and down for par only to aggravate the two peas in the pod. I was numb and really wasn't thinking about anything except my graduation, also known as the 18th hole.

The events on the front nine repeated themselves along with the Parrot and his narrations. J.J. Putz would stop by some tree so he could waste more time and stain the front of his pants. Piggy Pika kept pace by beating us on every other hole. He would make a few timely pars and net birdies when needed. By the time I got off the ninth hole I looked like I had been wrung out. I stopped at the bar.

"Kill anyone today?" May said.

"The day ain't over yet." I said repeating an exchange from the movie City Slickers.

May reloaded my cooler. I excused myself as I went to make room for more necessary alcohol. I had to squeeze into a bathroom that was declared too small by the Geneva Convention. I washed my hands and elbowed my way out germaphobe style.

I stopped at the bar to pick up my rations. "I should be back about 15 minutes before the cops get here. Maybe you can have a beer in a go-cup ready." I smiled.

"Be careful out there." May laughed.

I drove up to the 10th tee to join my new BFFs, "best friends for-never."   J.J. sat in my cart to go over the front nine scores with me.

I reviewed the card. "We lost the front nine but we did have 4 bippies."

"That's right, that's right; we had four bippies, don't forget, we had four bippies." Said guess who.

"I know, I know." J.J. said before he could catch himself.

"Contagious isn't it?" said Piggy. He laughed and something he was saving flew out of his mouth.

Cheap Bastard

I quickly covered my open beer with my left hand as I did the finances. They had beat us on the front nine, 1 down with no presses which means the Parrot and I were down $2 a man on the Nassau but we were up $4 on the bippies. So even though they beat us we were up $2 a man. I should say that Red Pika beat us but the back nine was different as the piglet had started to run out of steam.

We had them two-down after taking 10 and 11. On the 12th hole they really struggled off the tee.

"This is no good" The Putz yelled "I'm going to have to take a drop."

The Piggy was in the rough and nearly hopeless behind some bushes. The Parrot and I had them on the ropes.

"Okay" said The Piggy as he snap hooked his shot around the bushes landing safely in front of the green.

"A thirty-six handicap, you say?" I'm a little more than disgusted as I look toward my little Parakeet-like friend. "I am giving him two shots on this hole. If I make birdie I might tie him."

"I get two shots on this hole; too, I get two shots, too." As the Parrot repeated his repeat, "Two-too, get it?"

The Parrot hits his shot up and onto the cart path. It took two huge bounces and rolled up onto the green about two feet from the flag.

"I could kiss you." I said to the Parrot.

"Not bad for a 32, right? Not bad, right?"

"Not bad at all, Parrot, not bad at all." I shook my head wondering if we were all catching the habit.

The Putz-meister was of no help as he was on in four. He walked down the side of the hill to take another leak before returning to practice his unique putting skills. I was on in two but more than 15 feet away; a par would be no good here. I drained a worthless birdie as The Piggy got up and down for par net eagle. It was all up to the Parrot.

His hands were shaking so bad I wanted to pull him aside. He was just outside of two feet with a flat lie and a straight birdie putt. He took the putter back way too far for the purpose. Now he had to decelerate to make up for the huge backswing and hit the ground first and then the ball. He left the two-footer short by 14 inches.

"Hmph, phst, hmph, ahem" audible disgusting body sounds of joy were coming out of the piglet's pizza hole.

I think I heard those same sounds once before from the chiropractor at Brentwood. I wanted to smack him, as the Italians say, "upside the head." But the rules of golf are very strict about such things; if I damaged my putter I would have to take it out of play. The Parrot still shaken managed to tap the ball in to tie the hole.

"Good man" I said to the Parrot.

I turned to Piggy and said, "Laugh all you want, Pika, but you're still two down."

Pika laughed it off. He wasn't evil and he is still the Parrot's friend. He told the Parrot, "Good par by the way."

"Thanks, Thanks a lot."

Then on the 14th hole it all came to a head. The Putz was still lining up his third putt when the cart girl drove up some 40 yards away. She did not say a word but J.J. backed off trying to make it look like she's the reason he missed the first two putts.

"Do you mind!!?" He shouted at the girl.

The wind was howling off the bay and she could hardly hear him.

"Did you want something?" She yelled.

"Yes, I want you to GO AWAY! Get lost!" As he waved a regal disrespectful gesture as if to say, *"I am above you, leave my presence."*

The Parrot and I gave her an apologetic shrug and waved. She drove off with all of those wonderful overpriced $5 domestics. The Putz actually saved me money as I was already out of beer again.

He missed his 12 inch, 3rd putt and helicoptered the putter off the green toward the spot where the cart girl had been. Even the Parrot felt that this was a good time to be quiet. I was trying to think if this guy had any redeeming qualities; I actually thought of two: He made everyone around him look good and he gave us pleasure whenever he was not around. Even Piggy Pika shook his head back and forth in disgust; his own partner. Could there be a bigger insult than that? When we got to the next tee no one said a word so I broke the silence with my diplomacy.

"Hey Putz; I want you to know that this is the last time that I will ever play golf with you."

He turned his back to me and walked off the 15th tee, as he grabbed his hand cart and took giant steps toward the clubhouse. He was quitting.

"By the way, you're down $2 dollars. You can leave it at the bar. I'll pick it up later." I yelled.

"You really are a cheap bastard." said Pika.

"We all have our crosses." I shrugged

"Game off?" The Piggy asked.

"Yeah, sure. What do you say, Parrot?"

"Yeah, sure, you bet, you bet."

Aside from his bogus handicap and costume, Pika is a pretty decent sort. He equally complimented your good shots as he laughed at your bad ones. There is nothing phony about him. He is real but still I would not use him as a reference. Somewhere on his person there must be a calculator as he continued to manage his treasured 36 handicap. Unfortunately, he shot a 107 because he sunk a putt that I was sure he tried to lip out.

"They're going to post a 106 because you had an 8 on a par 4. You may drop to a 35." The Parrot calculated. Amazingly he did not repeat a single word.

"Yep, you may drop to a 35." He added after a little pause.

"Damn that Putz!" Red Pika cried, "And all for what?"

"Well you did save at least $2. You can owe me." I said.

He smiled at me. "Bets are off right?"

"Just kidding Pig but not for JJ. He still owes me $2."

"So next week then, next week?" chirped the Parrot. They were always teamed up in the same foursome.

"Yeah, sure."

"Yeah, sure."

I was so busy watching the action I did not realize my own game until I finished the 18th hole. I remember Artie telling me when he was stuck with the same group, he shot a 33-33 for a 66. Artie must have had a fast cart and a lot of Captain Morgan. He even managed to finish with the foursome intact; a moment that went down in the "anals" of our club history.

I had looked at the card and I had shot a 79; a miracle considering the constant bickering and aggravation.

"Nice round." said Pika.

"Yeah nice round, nice round."

As we walked toward the clubhouse all of the members were giving us a standing ovation. This ovation could have been for so many reasons but I tipped my hat as I felt it was part consolation and part compensation. I asked at the bar but the Putz never did leave me the two dollars so I called and left a message at his house. I heard someone behind me call me a "Cheap bastard" again

"Pig."

Pika said, "I didn't say anything. Besides you won; you have to buy me a beer."

"Oh good grief!"

** Golf is like all bad habits; the best way to quit is not to take it up in the first place. **

4: Get Out of Town

Timing Really Is Everything

The year we moved into the Fort Lauderdale area, the Yankees moved spring training to Tampa and the local annual PGA tournament went north. Everyone was leaving town as my wife and I were coming in. There should have been a message but it fell to deaf ears; we are living in Florida! "What could be better?" you ask. How about free stuff?!

I really am a cheap bastard. I was born of Celtic descent and married a Jewish girl to further hone my frugal skills. I happened to join an over-expensive country club because, well frankly, my office was paying for it.

Most people call our club "the Lakes" because "The Lakes at Fairview Country Club" is a freakin' mouthful. The only people who use the full name would be real estate agents or over-bearing pretentious sales people but then I repeat myself (with the exception of my good friend, Diane, I did not mean her of course).

The very first day I went to the Lakes I went as a guest of our company president, Ed Jackson. Ed is a big man. It is not just his six foot six inch frame; he was once a football player and most likely a descendant of a Maine lobster. When you shake hands with Ed you can only stretch your fingers across half of his bone crushing palm. I felt like a five year old shaking a grown-up's catcher's mitt. It is extremely embarrassing but I guess he lives with it.

"We inherited the membership here when we bought SudCo." Ed mentioned. "They had had a membership here since they opened this place in eighty-two." Ed was obviously a history buff.

"Looks very nice." I said, trying to play it nonchalant.

"You know, I was thinking. I live all the way in Nebraska. What's the point of me having a membership here? Why don't I sign it over to you? You'll get more use out of it and I can always come as a guest when I'm in town!"

Okay nonchalant left town with my tongue as I mustered, "Uh… uh, oh, oh, okay!"

Ed laughed at my stuttering excitement, "A fine speaker you are."

If my speaking skills did not impress him my golf game might have helped; if only my hands would stop shaking.

Ed selected a one-iron out of his bag. I didn't know anyone that still carried one. He had a driver but it looked like it never cleared leather. I mean, it still had the price tag on it.

"You don't use your driver?"

"No" Big Ed waved a hand and brushed one of the clouds away, "I always hook the damned thing."

He teed it up and took a violent practice swing before he took an even more violent real thrash at his ball. The ball started out over the driving range to the right; it hooked left across the entire fairway.

"Stop, stop! Sit! Settle! Settle!" He begged and screamed and stop it did, in the left rough short of the water.

"Whew, that was close!" He said, almost exhausted from cheering for his ball.

"And you say you hook your driver?" I squeezed out before thinking.

"Yeah, well, worse than that."

Still, he hit that ball about two-hundred twenty yards; by my calculations it probably traveled well over three-fifty if it had gone straight. Now it was my turn. I don't take a practice swing unless I have a short shot so I think I surprised Ed when I just got up and hit it. I smoked it down the middle much to my surprise considering I still had the shakes.

"You get much work done in between golf, do you?" Ed asked while closing one eye and inspecting me with the other.

I laughed, "That was only my first shot. My handicap hasn't kicked in yet."

I hadn't known Ed too long. He had joined our company shortly before the purchase of SudCo. He came right in as president and no one questioned his credentials. I don't think anyone ever questioned Big Ed unless they were suicidal. I was a VP in a long line of VPs. I had the biggest company project at that time so he got to know me very quickly. If not for this good timing I'd be looking at the Lakes Club from outside the fence.

Ed and I finished our round, had a few drinks and took our wives to dinner later that night. He repeated his offer of the club in front of my wife which was good because I thought that maybe I had dreamt the whole thing. Suddenly I felt very successful and that scared the shit out of me as Jack whispered a consoling message.

** Now you really have something to lose. **

"I should be back in town in a few weeks. We can get some golf in and I'd like to try the Blue Monster, if you are up for it?" Ed was rhetorical.

I answered anyway, "Sure. Just let me know when so I can buy more golf balls."

The Blue Monster is part of Miami's Dural Country Club. It is over $300 to play there and a one-shot bloody mary in a Styrofoam cup goes for a fast $20. The whole concept of that place goes against my grain unless someone else is buying.

Our company was in over 200 countries around the world. As it turned out Ed's travels would never let him make it back to the Lakes. I would see him when we crossed paths at different places and our conversations always went like this:

"How's the project? More importantly, how's the golf game?"

"Great and terrible." I'd reply.

"I hope that's respectively." he'd laugh as loud as his size would dictate and I'd laugh in comparison which is more like a snicker.

I would keep that Lakes membership for more than twelve short years. As each year went by, I watched it change ownership and management. We lost our great greenskeeper and the course spiraled downhill quickly. Say what you will about George Steinbrenner but he put his money back into his club. We needed a George to own the Lakes. This is why the PGA moved the tournament and maybe why the Yankees left. They knew. You've-got-to-have-a-game Bob, Jimmy-the-two and I kept playing. Jimmy-the-two is named for his handicap. Bob is called Bob because his name is Robert.

"They stopped mowing the primary rough to save a buck." Bob said as we tried to find my ball.

"This place is a goat ranch." Jim added his own complaint.

It wasn't always that way. The course was once the jewel of South Florida; like any golf course it is a reflection of the owner.

You Remind Me of the Man

Before the course went downhill it was spectacular. Plush greens, manicured first and second cut of rough and tightly mowed fairways. It's a tough course with out of bounds on one side and lakes on the other.

My first day as a member of the Lakes was a perfect fall day with low humidity and 78 degrees. Puffy clouds rolled in and out of blue skies and a light breeze kept everything comfortable. I got a tee time and I was paired with a few strangers. The most notable of them was John.

The game was unimportant to John; he didn't even hit one ball at the range. He waited at the bar....no, no, no, let me rephrase that; he pounded down beer after beer until it was our time to tee off. He had me pick him up at the bar and drive right to the first tee. His clubs were a matched set of scratched woods and scarred irons. Good stuff but not a head cover in the bunch.

John got up without even a practice swing, hit the ball and nearly fell but the ball went down the middle about 50 yards. He did better on his second shot and that's the way he played; alternating bad shots with terrific shots throughout the day. He hovered under 100 shots but he never held anyone up. How could he? Without a single practice swing or hesitation he would hit the ball, fix his divot and get back in the cart with his club and his beer. He'd even bring his putter to the cart after we finished the hole. I looked at him and the club.

Reading my expression he pointed out what was obvious to him, "Saves time."

"How's that?" Not quite sure what he meant.

"I take the club in the cart because I will be going to my bag again for the next shot. Why go twice to the bag when once will do; saves time."

The logic was inescapable so I said, "Very true. The beer does not affect you at all, does it?"

"Only if it's empty." He laughed. "Actually I get to a certain high and then it's only a matter of maintenance."

John stood just less than 6 feet, just under 60 years old and just under the weather. He had a distinguished salt and pepper load of hair and a constant grin as if he knew something you didn't. He owned a corner of the bar that was reserved for him and his generous tips. The staff loved him and so does everyone who knows him.

He drank Coors Light on ice and he had nearly a full case while I was with him. The cart girl never passed us by without stopping to reload John's belly and mine. It had no impact on him. He was already well-lit when we started; and I joined him as part of the "maintenance" crew. I've been known to polish off a twelve pack on the course but I could not keep up with the likes of John. It was not for the lack of trying. After 18 holes of lightening the beverage cart we gave our clubs to the boys downstairs. John over tipped them with a 10 spot so I only gave them my $2 figuring that $12 was plenty for them. We hurried up the stairs into the bar before the buzz wore off.

*** Cheap Bastard! ***

"What did you shoot today, John?" someone in locker room asked.

"About 12 silver bullets on ice." John smiled out of the more sober side of his mouth.

"And that was before the first tee." I added.

We sat at the bar and made snide and nasty comments under our breath about every female that sauntered, swayed, played or walked by. We laughed so hard that tears fell from our eyes about who knows what. John had asked me to join his regular group.

"Sometimes we have only three; sometimes we are six and split into two groups. Would you like to join us Saturday?"

"I'd love it. Do you think that either of us will remember this conversation?"

"Probably not but you can reintroduce yourself on Saturday." John said, "By the way, what did you shoot?"

"Damned if I know, I left the scorecard in the cart" I must have sounded like Foster Brooks.

"Good" John said." At least we can enjoy our lunch."

And then I realized who he reminded me of.

More Family Affairs

The thought of John reminded me of the things I missed about my younger days. I remembered the company picnics my dad brought me to. There was the smell of hot dogs, hamburgers and corn roasting on the charcoal grills with too much lighter fluid that overpowered the taste. My early experience and thin stature taught me to be patient and wait for the second round. The lines were too long anyway. Like my dad I liked my meat barely cooked. So I would bide my time with a Coke or two. There were these galvanized garbage pails filled with ice, beer and soda. Your arm would freeze trying to reach for your beverage of choice. It took me several attempts as I picked beer after beer from the frozen depths. Later in life when I wanted a beer the process would reverse itself as if it were in Jack's plan.

** This is just you're kind of luck but I'll be happy to take the credit. **

Finally, yes finally, the food line was empty and the coals were red and clear. "Can I get a burger rare; you know, barely cooked."

"You'll get worms!"

"Thanks but I'll take my chances. I just don't like well-done chop meat."

"Okay. It's your funeral."

"Mister, are you a golfer, by any chance?"

75

"No, kid. Here you go."

"Thanks."

"Don't eat that too fast now."

"Yes sir. "I said and I thought as I walked away "I don't care what he says, he's an *advice toad* straight from New Hampshire."

I considered this worthless exchange just plain stupid but it was well worth the wait. And although it does not seem to apply this relates to golf as well. If you have to lean awkwardly over a short putt to finish, you might want to mark it and wait. Missing a short putt is like too much lighter fluid; it stinks and leaves a bad taste in your mouth. Patience in golf is not only a weapon; it is an arsenal. However, this is not an excuse for slow play.

Back at the picnic I watched my dad. He was a great ball player and I watched him play softball at the picnic, that is, for about two minutes, maybe. I never got to play ball with my dad but I got to play with my kids for a few years. They stumbled a bit in the early teens but surpassed me very quickly. The level of play turned from my strength to theirs in a few years, and finally I had to hang up my spikes. Golf has more longevity but my boys have no interest in the game. They are, after all, far more intelligent than I.

Hawaii Japanese Style

Hawaii is still a magical place even if it has been over developed. There are plenty of pseudo-Polynesian activities contrived by half-Hawaiian, half Japanese people who call this home. We've been there a few times but I've never seen a real luau. You know the ones you see on TV where you sit on the sand in a circle around a roasted pig wrapped in banana leaves and you eat with your hands off a wooden plate while you get lei' d. What you usually get is a plastic knife and fork with a drink in a plastic cup. Hula dancers twirl fire-batons around a pool on a cement patio. Someone pre-roasts a pig and you buffet your way to the tasteless paste they call poi. If you are actually on the beach you fill your paper plate and sit at a picnic table with a plastic table cloth. Once, in Maui my wife and I sat in the sand; the tables were full. The one thing they cannot bastardize is the weather. There are no snakes, no mosquitos, not a single poisonous plant and you are comfortable in a tee shirt all year round. If you want a less commercial, more Polynesian experience you best go to the outer islands.

They say that there are more Japanese people in Hawaii than any other nationality including the natives. Many of them are very successful. My buddy Dennis once said, "If they had only waited 50-60 years, they could have bought the place."

The Pearl Harbor museum is a must see and surprisingly many Japanese visit as well. The Arizona memorial is a place of respectful silence. The only break from the silence is a speech from George Bush (the smart one; not his son). He had recorded a message for us to *remember* but to also *put aside our differences*. It is a good speech and necessary before someone forgets, yells Banzai and throws someone overboard.

My wife and I took up a round at the Prince Country Club where we got paired with a Japanese couple. In the spirit of Bush's words we let them bow while we shook their hands. As it turned out, Aina (Ah-eee-na), the wife, could not speak any English at all. Daichi (Di-chee), the husband, spoke very little English but we managed to communicate. There was a lot of bowing and nodding and then they would talk to each other like they were ordering sushi.

Aina was a petite 5 foot dark haired, *I was once a geisha* looking girl of about 40 years of age. She was dressed all in white except for her pink belt and shoes. Daichi seemed to be a well off businessman. He was a head taller than his wife but about the same age. He looked efficiently powerful, well-disciplined and physically fit; everything he wore said Nike. He had a white shirt but everything else was navy blue, even his shoes.

They played at about the same level as we did and when they hit a good shot I would tell them so. He would say, "Domo" which I figured out. I hit a few good drives and Daichi, would say, "eee – barl, eee- barl." The 'l' was pretty much silent but it was there. I figured 'barl' was 'ball'.

"What does this mean, eee-barl?" I asked.

Aina started to laugh, I guess at my poor Japanese pronunciation and then Stephanie joined her and now both girls were hysterical.

"I guess the joke is on me." I laughed.

*** Isn't it always? ***

Daichi laughed too but then he started to explain, "Eee- barl; eee is good, good barl" and then he held up a golf ball, "barl. Eee-barl; …good barl… good, good…" and then he found the words, "good shot!"

"Oh thank you, thank you…I mean, domo" and I bowed and then he bowed. I got in the cart and Stephanie had still not recovered. They got in their cart and chuckled down the path.

"Okay, it was funny but it wasn't that funny." I asked more than I said.

Steph was still out of control. I had to slow the cart down so she could regain her composure. I let them get a lead down the path.

I repeated "It wasn't *that* funny. I must have pronounced it wrong", I paused, and "I guess she thought it was funny."

Steph could barely get the words out, "She was laughing and then," Steph wiped a tear from her eye and she struggled with the words, "She was laughing and then it hit me, "Laughing Ah-eee-na"."

I immediately slowed the cart down before someone Samurai-d our ass.

Daichi and I exchanged eee-barls until we got to this one hole where I hit my tee shot into the lava. I turned to Daichi and asked, "How do you say "bad shot"?"

"Shit!" he said and pronounced it perfectly.

The laughter erupted again as Stephanie fell out the cart.

"She does that a lot." I said.

After 18 holes of bowing, nodding and laughing we decided to get lunch. I really wanted sushi but I was afraid that my translation might cause another eruption so we ate at the club. After we were done, we said our good-byes, with unending bows and exchanged phone numbers. This was ludicrous because how could we communicate on the phone. Every time I spoke to Daichi I must have sounded like Tonto. But taking each other's cards seemed obligatory and we waved goodbye with a smile forever.

"Nice couple. What did you think of them, Jack?"

** *I noticed that your speaking louder did not help in the translation process.* **

Take a Cruise

I'm not mentioning any names here so let's just say there was this cruise; a seven day cruise. Sailing the Caribbean can be very entertaining but let's face it, a boat of any size can be confining. Most people think of the ports they will arrive at and the excursions. If you opt to see a port on your own, you better boogie your ass down to the tender, hit landfall like a marine, see what you came to see, collect something and get your ass back to the ship before it takes off. I know I am being a little unfair but, if you think you can book a tee time and get back to the ship you will be looking at your watch from the second tee on. Unless you are on a cruise specifically wrapped around golf, don't even bother bringing your clubs.

All that aside, there is always that "one full day at sea" and passengers are starved for entertainment. But no worries, mate, most cruise ships have a little golf experience at the stern of the ship. If golf is your entire life, I'll fill you in; *the stern is in the back*. The crew has a bunch of golf balls, a driver and a long line of golfers. They are impatient; each rubbing their index finger like a saw across their nose and scratching at their forearms like addicts waiting for a hit.

As they waited many of them practiced their grip with an invisible club. From a distance they looked like they were peeing off the starboard side or on each other.

There were plenty of golf balls so each person would get to hit four balls. This is a treat because usually you only get three. It also takes a little longer so patience was thinning. Despite the crew's assurance the 50 mathematically-challenged could be seen leaning over to count the number of balls left and then their position in line. About mid-way through the line, the 22nd person took the driver, teed up the ball and took his sole practice swing. That was really all that was needed. The reason was because the person taking that practice swing was already warmed up by the sun and all of that wonderful suntan lotion. Blue Coppertone 30 was to blame for the club that slipped through those well-oiled hands right off the stern of the ship and into that beautiful deep Caribbean

"Oh Shit!!"

A gigantic gasp was heard. Oh, did I mention that this was the only golf club aboard the ship. Loud muttering followed, you know, the threatening kind.

"Hey, the drinks are on me!"

This comment was the only thing that saved this guy from being thrown off the back to retrieve the club. Once again, I'll not mention any names to save any undue further embarrassment.

** *Asshole.* **

"It wasn't me, Jack. It was this guy I know."

** *Yeah, right. I'm with ya'.* **

Kiss the Blarney Stone

Probably one of the most expensive things I've ever done without my wife was to go to Ireland. You don't need to lay any guilt trip on me, I do fine all on my own. And then, of course there is always Jack

** *Right here for you baby!* **

One of the guys at the club that I played with every weekend was forming a trip to Ireland. Seven days on 5 courses in the south of Ireland. A five star hotel, gourmet meals, a 57 passenger bus for only 8 guys all ready to drink, eat, drink and play golf, tell disgusting jokes while we drank some more, puke like a bulimic and then wash it all down with some Guinness Stout with an Irish Whisky chaser. Paul needed 8 golfers and after we had six great guys that enjoyed each other's company we must have expanded the draft requirements. Nothing else could explain the unbalanced chemistry.

Just being in Ireland is exceptional but we also happened to have two very well-respected doctors with us: a renowned cardiologist who also was called upon to operate on apes and a brilliant orthopedic surgeon who limited his practice to humans. This was handy in case of a sudden heart issue, a broken bone or a hangover.

We also had a mortgage broker, an investment counselor and an investment swindler in case you had a little money or too much money. Then we had a psychiatrist for those special golf emotions and lastly an Indian salesman; he himself was not Indian he was actually a purveyor of offshore souls. I brought Jack with me because he had never been to Ireland and I really have no choice in the matter.

** There is no way I am going to miss all of these wonderful opportunities. **

"Bastard!"

** Ah, hah, hah, hah. ** I heard his playfull laugh of pleasure and then it faded away.

We all had to book our own airfare and then meet at Shannon airport on Sunday. Tomas, the surgeon, and I took off the day before to stay overnight in London. These were the days when he had so many freakin' flyer miles we flew first class. We flew Virgin Atlantic on Tomas' free miles and I gave him mine to use for another trip he was taking. Tomas is a big 6 foot 5 inch guy and looked more like a football lineman than a doctor.

We would have trouble if we were in coach but we had no problems on one of Richard Branson's first class operations. These were not just fist class lounge seats these would fold flat down like beds with blankets, pillows, and round-the-clock wining and dining.

** I could get used to this! **

"Me too."

"Me too what?" Tomas said.

"I could get used to this!" I said.

"Oh yeah, me too." Tomas answered.

And we washed down some warm nuts with vodka and beer as they walked through with cheese, goose liver pate, truffles and caviar.

** Anyone for the gout platter? **

Tomas and I pretended to be nonchalant but snagged a few items and then a few more like it was last call. She smiled even though she had to return to the kitchen to refill the platter.

"I'll be right back." Tomas said as he got up. He went to make some more room for desert.

I can always tell when Jack is around, the air seems a little bit colder, the hairs on my arms stand up and my shoulders creep up to my neck. It is like someone just dropped an ice cube down my back.

** There are other passengers you know! ** Jack imitated a flight attendant; a pissed off flight attendant, you know like the ones back there in coach.

"Do you want some?" I whispered to Jack.

** Very funny, shmuck. **

"You on a diet? Are you watching your ectoplasm maybe?"

** Oh, you're going to pay for that one. Oh how you're going to pay! **

"Yeah , yeah, save me a seat you bastard."

** Oh it's reserved, buddy; it's reserved. **

85

Tomas came back and I said, "My turn; be right back."

"Wait until you see the head." Tomas pointed.

I expected the usual room but there was room for a mile-high initiation for 2 couples in there. There were real cloth towels, real toilet paper, powder, cologne and you name it. I washed up and got back to Tomas. At least Jack let me have one place in solitude.

"I could not believe that bathroom! I mean on a plane?"

"Unbelievable, right?" Tomas shrugged.

"I've been in first class before but this is way beyond that."

I was afraid to go to sleep and miss something. I was thinking of asking Tomas to sleep in shifts. I knew Jack would be of no help on purpose.

I could hear him, *Wow, you should have seen what you missed while you were sleeping? Lobsters, king crab, oysters…."*

But the food, the wine and airtime made me sleepy and I could hold on no longer.

"I'm going to hit the hay, Tomas."

"Yeah, me too. This movie's on for about ten more minutes but I may be asleep before the end."

Of course we each had our own TV, I hit the off button and it folded up and disappeared. I reclined my seat into a bed and started to pull the covers up. The flight attendant came over, asked if we needed anything else as she handed me a bottle of water, a pair of blinders and some sleeping slippers.

"Oh, thank you very much."

Tomas said. "Thank you."

** That'll be all then miss; on your way now! **

"Good night."

"Good night."

**Good night. **

The cabin was dark enough. I tried the blinders but they weren't for me. I do not remember closing my eyes; they just opened to hear people drowning out the sound of the wind.

"Good morning. Would you like some coffee?" She said as she handed me a menu.

"Yes, thank you." I looked over and Tomas was already up and was eating some eggs benedict and fresh melon."

"I think I'm dreaming. Oh and good morning."

"Good morning. Most comfortable flight I've ever had. We should be landing in Gatwick within the hour. I got us a pretty decent hotel outside the airport. We can grab some dinner around town and see some local stuff. We fly out to Shannon in the morning so we won't be able to see much."

"Maybe we can just fly around in this plane."

"Sounds good to me."

Gatwick Quick

The only downside of a stopover is having to wheel your luggage through customs from the airport only to reverse the process tomorrow. A big suitcase, golf clubs and a back pack over one shoulder is a struggle but two elevator rides and a taxi found us safely there. The hotel bellhop let us keep the clubs down stairs at least.

Tomas had a plan. "How about we take a shower, get a drink at the hotel bar and head down the street; maybe we can find a local place to have dinner."

"Sounds good to me." I agreed.

*** You keep using that phrase. Should I call the parrot and tell him it's normal? ***

" Go ahead."

"Okay." Tomas shrugged as he stepped ahead and entered the elevator first.

Most people fly into Heathrow and head right for Piccadilly Square, the Tower of London or the Jack the Ripper tour; not us, this was only a stopover. We found the hotel unimpressive after Virgin Atlantic but we met at the bar which was pretty fancy for the place. I had a Bass Ale and Tomas sipped their best vodka on the rocks. The bartender was a skinny man with black hair. It was clear that neither he nor his hair had ever seen the sun. His manner was stiff and pompous.

*** I'm pretty sure he sleeps in a coffin during the day. ***

"You gents need anything else." He stated as a fact rather than a question.

"Yes, thank you.   We're from out of town (obviously) and we were wondering if there was some local pub within walking distance where we might get a bite to eat. "

"We have a very fine restaurant right here in the hotel. Would you like to see the menu." Again not a question but stated as if there were no choice.   He handed us two menus before we could respond.

*** I hate pressure salespeople.   I think the British accent makes it worse. ***

I looked sideways at Jack's voice and then back to the bartender. "I'm sure it is but this is our only night here and we're off to Shannon in the morning so…"

"Oh I see." The bartender cut me off.

*** You just told a Brit he's only a side trip to Ireland, asshole. ***

Jack was right. The bartender felt obliged to give us some directions through the nicest part of town. We walked through this neighborhood. The houses looked small but well-kept except the occasional neglected variety where a couple of thugs were hanging out. Tomas is an educated medical man and as I said he is also a big man especially walking next to me. Tomas is not violent but then, who would know? A few teenagers looked our way but then walked the other. I guess they figured if we were crazy enough to walk here they wanted no part of us.

We saw only a few more street thug Clockwork Orange types before we got to what looked like Main Street. We approached one pub but if the door did not stop us the smell did. It was like old shoes left in a wet basement soaked in last week's chicken fat. The next one was the same minus the chicken. It seemed they would all be that way.

"I'm thinking we should have eaten at the hotel." Tomas said.

"Wait! "The Golfer's Tee, Steak and Ale", I read out load.

The smells from the kitchen flew out the front door and carrying waves of freshly cooked steak and laughter.

"Let's sit at the bar and look at the menu." I suggested.

** *Good thing you had a 'u' at the end of that sentence.* **

"Oh, very funny, jerk!"

** *Homophobe.* ** Jack always seems to get the last word.

"Perfect." Tomas seemed a bit warn out too. "My feet are tired and I'd like to try an English beer myself."

"Try the Bass Ale, if nothing else." I suggested as we stooled up to the bar.

** Stooled?   What?   Did you drop a load? ** Jack attacked. ***Poetic license, aside.   Sat, saddled up, ponied up, leaned on; so many choices. You chose "stooled"? ***

"Fine! We took a seat at the bar."

** Nice out. **

"You gents are from the States, are you not?   The bartender's accent was hard to place.

"Yes."

"Me too. My name is Greg." the guy next to Tomas said. "I'm from New Hampshire. I flew in from Miami, though."

"So did we! Well, we're from the Fort Lauderdale area really, but we just flew in from Miami.   I spent a lot time in New Hampshire as a kid." I added.

** We're not going to suffer another tortured little leaguer story, are we? **

I gave Jack the finger as I rubbed my eye but I kept quiet.

"Want to join us for dinner?" Tomas offered.

"Sure."

We had a second drink on the bartender and exchanged our names. We looked at a great menu with local food. We exchanged golf stories and a third round before the waitress showed us our table. She returned to take our order.

"The House Steak and Ale here is our specialty." She was overly cheerful but it was honest and seemed to be her way.

Greg said. "I think I'll have that this evening."

"Aren't you worried about the Mad Cow?" Tomas warned.

"Nah." Greg said, "That's a bunch of hype, besides, she's home at the hotel."

Everyone laughed except the waitress for some reason but then, like a grenade, she and her blonde hair finally got it. She said, "Oh, that's good one, that is!"

"Hmmm, Okay. Steak and ale. I'll have that too." Tomas said.

"That sounds good to me, too." I figured if Tomas is having it, it must be okay.

"The news media could turn a wolf into a vegan." Greg said.

"How long have you been here? You're beginning to sound like a local." I joked with Greg.

"Too long; way too long but there's some good golf around all of England. I am sure you'll have plenty of it in Ireland. I moved here nearly two years ago. I pick a spot, live it for two years and move on to the next. My dad was from here and next is Edinburg where my mom grew up, France is next. Yes sir; just me, my clubs and my golf partner. I got a new set of triple RZX I29 G's." But Greg seemed juxtaposed; obviously a wealthy man stuck in a helpless path, he added. "My wife still beats me by seven strokes."

"Where is she now?" Tomas asked.

"Practicing." Greg's said. The sun positioned itself against his diamond studded Rolex Presidential and nearly blinded me.

*** Thou shall not covet they neighbor's goodies. ***

Contrary to anything you may hear about England the food can be spectacular. It was a little overdone for my rare preference but very tasty. Greg drove us back to the hotel.

"You may think we will not see each other again but I seem to run into people time and time again." Greg said. "So I'm not saying goodbye; I'll say, "See you later.""

We said our farewell and Tomas and I reflected on Greg's company. "I bet he's good to be with on the golf course."

"For sure."

We headed to our rooms nearly worn out from the trip; I could barely wash up. Thank God we did not have to walk back to the hotel. Tomorrow we would have a short flight but a very full day.

Shannon

Tomas and I met in the lobby with more luggage then two people should. We loaded them up with a very small and very unhappy cab driver. We headed to the airport bound for Ireland. As the cabby drove on and thought about his tip his demeanor became nearly human.

Security was tight as expected but we got through. I felt like we had not reached altitude when we started coming down.

"Short trip" Tomas shrugged.

"Hope so." I replied.

** Chicken shit. **

About half the boys were there when we got to the bar at Shannon Airport. It was a good place to gather the troops. I looked over at the bar and this one gray-haired guy was teetering over a bar stool and then he fell down.

** That's probably your bus driver. **

"I hope that's no our bus driver." I said as everyone laughed; everyone but Jack that is.

** You haven't a lick of wit of your own do you? **

I shrugged it off. I don't often get the better of Jack so I sipped the last of my beer with a grin. We ordered another round which came just as the rest of our guys came around the corner.

4: Get out of Town

Paul and his 6 feet 7 inch frame were not hard to spot. He is a giant in every way. Hands, head, legs and forearms are like a football player but he never played. "Hey guys looks like everyone's here except the bus driver."

Everyone repeated the story of the drunk as I thought I felt a smack in the back of my head. It was only the waitress squeezing by.

"Sorry, 'bout dat."

"Sorry." I said as I moved my chair closer to the table.

A more sober man approached us; he was about my height and build but he and his clothes had 10 years on me. His thick brogue was tough to understand but you get the meaning like a grenade. You realized what he had said but it took about five seconds.

*** He just thinks you're slow. Most people have to get to know you first. ***

He introduced himself as Patty or Patrick whichever we liked; made no difference to him. The bus was a 57-passenger monster with the steering wheel, as we American say, "On the wrong side." It had that greyhound look to it but surprisingly it had no bathroom. Still a big bus for 8 passengers seemed like overkill.

"So tell me, Wayne is it?"

"Yes, sir."

"Patty." He said.

"Okay, Patty it is then." Trying a bit of a brogue myself.

"Tell me, Wayne, wared' ar' ya frim in the states?"

"Well we all flew in from Miami but I'm from a place in New York called Long Island."

"Long Island! I know da' place! I 'ave a coozin dare I bet maybe ya' know 'em?"

"Well Patty, Long Island is a big big place with millions of people. I doubt that…"

"'is name is Rick Duffy."

"Not Rick Duffy from Islip?" I said with my eyes wide open.

"Aye, dat would be 'im."

"And his wife's name is Kate?"

"Aye."

"They live across the street from me, or they did when I lived there."

"So dis Long Island, it is not such a big place after all, is it! I mentioned one name an 'e lives across the street!" And he told that story to everyone we met. "Oh sure; it's a big place…" and the story got bigger and Long Island sounded smaller each time he told it. And Jack laughed every single freakin' time at my expense.

*** You've got to love the Irish. ***

And I do love the Irish and they do love Americans. It seems every one of them has an aunt, an uncle, a nephew or a cousin in the "States" as they call it. They have many stories to tell and they are all spiced with colorful expressions and topped with a fine accent. They say 67% of the country is made up of alcoholics.

** *You'd blend in nicely here.* ** Jack pointed out.

"I certainly will Ollie." I said.

I was kidding Jack with a Laurel and Hardy reference.

** *Funny, now scratch the top of your head and grin like an idiot. I'd hardly call that acting.* **

The bus delivered us from the airport to the hotel via the 'wrong' side of the road. I sat up front near Patty in the beginning but then moved back a seat or two. It was, hmmm, disconcerting.

** *One again, chicken!* **

The hotel was just outside of Killarney. It was spectacular. A large 3 story tan brick building with circular stone driveway, white horse fencing around a giant green piece of property on a beautiful lake. There is something about the water that takes your breath away. I know; I play golf. Water will do that to you.

"We'll be staying here all week" Paul said. "Patty will pick us up each morning and take us to each course."

"Except Thursday, right?" Bobby asked.

"Right, Bobby. Thursday we take a helicopter to Old Head. They'll pick us up right here on the front lawn. Tomorrow we play Ballybunion. We'll eat early and be out of here by 7:00 in the morning."

"And this affects me how?" Steve said.

Steve Madeoff looks too much like Bill Clinton which is annoying enough. As you get to know Steve better you realized what an insult this really is to Clinton. He has this deep southern accent beneath a fine crop of cotton colored hair.

Patty asked, "Ware' arrr ya' frim Steve?"

"Al La Bamma?" Steve made it sound like a three word question but that's his way.

Patty looked at me and asked, "Dat's in da states right?"

"Yes, sir, I mean, Patty."

Paul said, "I want to remind you that every round we will have a caddy and you have to walk the course. I hope you guys brought a carry-bag to keep the caddies happy."

"And this affects me how?" Steve said.

Paul wrapped his left palm and fingers like a skull cap over Steve's reddening head. "Shut up, Steve."

Steve probably would have said something but he had to catch his breath after Paul released him.

*** Please Steve, tells us how that affected you. ***

We split company at the elevator as we each had our own huge room overlooking the lake. I had Steve on one side of me and Tomas on the other. I knew that because we were all leaning on our balconies at the same time with the drink of our choice. Tomas had his vodka, I had my Guinness and Steve had an umbrella in his drink.

I leaned over to Tomas and said, "I think he goes out of his way to find things to piss us off."

Tomas mocked, "And this affects me how?"

Steve leaned over, 'Hey what's all the laughter about."

"Planning on taking that umbrella to the golf course?" I teased him to hide our secret.

Each morning we had a buffet breakfast or we could order something special from the kitchen. The buffet was nicely laid out so we ate there which was part of the deal. Steve ordered a special breakfast every day of course.

"Try the bacon." I offered to Steve.

Steve waved me off, "Too much of that stuff'll kill ya', rait Aaron."

'Yes, it sure will, Steve" and Aaron added. "Don't forget to order some sausage with that."

We all looked at each other and laughed; well not everybody.

*** Nobody is truly worthless; they can always be used as a poor example. ***

Ballybunion

We took off for Ballybunion on time and it was drizzling a little.

"I've got my Gortex and a rain hat with me just in case." I said.

"Got that umbrella?" Tomas asked Steve.

"And this affects me how?"

** *Somebody please press a soft pillow on his face for about 5 minutes.* **

We were allowed to smoke on the bus so my cigars took me to the back where Bobby was having a cigarette. Steve did not like the smoke so we made sure to keep the repelling fog going.

Bobby was about my size but much thinner. Like Tomas he was born in Cuba but neither of them has an accent. He shaved his head, had no mustache, no beard and was very tan. He's good company on and off the course and we sat in the back laughing and smoking until we got to the famous Ballybunion.

I had to get rid of breakfast to make room for some more beer and put on my Gortex so I excused myself. When I came out all of the guys had selected their caddies. I saw this skinny bit of a guy in black rain gear. He was the only one left so I said, "I guess you're with me."

The caddy spun around and said, "Hi, my name is Sabrina."

She was young, maybe 22, jet black hair tucked under her hat and behind her collar. She had some freckles to remain Irish and looked like a runner. She had only a hint of an accent here and there. Funny about impressions but now that I realized that she was a girl she seemed taller.

"Don't worry, I'm twenty-four and I bin' caddyin' since I was fit-teen. My father's the greenskeeper here for twenty years and I know this course better than any of the ithers. You listen to me, hit it where I tell ya' and ya' will score well here." Her confidence was unshakeable as she picked up my bag and slung it over her shoulder like it weighed nothing. I doubt that she weighed much over 100 herself.

We practiced a bit, mostly putting and chipping, as the caddies grouped together to watch and make their side bets.

I looked at the map of the first hole and looked up. Most of the green and the fairway were hidden but it dog-legged to the right. Sabrina told me where to hit it but I had my own ideas and paid the price. Had I hugged the left side I would have bounded to the middle. Instead I am deep in the rough and hacked my way into a double bogey. From that point on I did not make a move without Sabrina's approval. I could not hit it as accurately as she might have liked but I was close enough the keep the ball in play. She seemed to grasp what I could and could not do very quickly. Hell, I don't even know what I can and cannot do. I still don't

I looked at this one hole and what she told me defied all the logic my eyes could gather.

"Ya see those red booshes on the left?"

"Okay."

"I want you to hit the ball right at 'em wit' a 7 iron."

"What? Okay, okay, I trust you."

Everyone else in my group hit a driver to what looked like the middle. It looked pretty good to me but when we got over the hill there was only one ball in the fairway. Sabrina headed right for that ball.

"That can't be mine. I don't hit a 7 iron 200 yards!"

"Oh that's you alright. Ya' see the left part of that fairway and how it bends straight down from those red bushes. I figured you to carry that iron 150 and it shot another fifty down the hill like a pro. Your friends had to clear 240 and none of them made it. Let's go help them look. I figure them to be about ten yards ahead of you in the rough." The rough was light on that side and the balls were found easily. Some were hittable; Bobby needed to take a drop.

"I should have listened to my caddy." Bobby said.

"I haven't made a move without mine since the second hole. They know the course a lot better than we do."

When the round was over I shot a 77 and it was totally Sabrina's doing. The rain had stopped somewhere around the 7th hole. Bobby and I decided to go back out and play their new course. Bobby's caddy and Sabrina carried our bags for the second 18. We were enjoying the day when we hit a log jam at the first par three. Sabrina said these guys are alone and if we jump past them and skip this hole we would be in hours before them.

Bobby and I said okay and Sabrina took off running with my bag. The three of us could not catch up to her until she stopped.

"I run 10 miles every morning." Sabrina said.

"That explains a lot."

After a few holes we caught our breath on a par 5. I said to Sabrina, "Okay where should I hit this one."

"You see that bunker on the right."

"Yeah. I see it." I said.

"If you hit it in that bunker, you and I will be stuck in there for a week."

"Okay, where should I hit it?"

She looked at me with a smile and a shrug. "Hit it in that bunker." And then she laughed.

"Okay."

"No, no, no; anywhere on the left will do just fine." She said.

Bobby said, 'That was cute. I figured that flattery probably increased her tip by a few Euros." Bobby and I laughed.

Sabrina looked at us and we let her in on the conversation. She laughed and then she said, "I already made quite a bit wit' Mr. Martin. You see I won the bet with the ither caddies. I'll still take a big tip though."

Cheap bastard that I am I broke from tradition and gave her twice the normal amount for the day. You see, she was not the only one who won. I basically split my winnings with her which seemed only fair. Sabrina introduced me to her dad, Scott, who looked about my age. He was smaller than me but the bones of my hands cried when he shook my hand. They were calloused stones that shook my molars.

"Did she give ya' an advantage o'er da rest of your mates?" His accent was thick.

"Aye." I said. "I played better than I ever played because I listened to Sabrina." I was getting into the brogue of things.

"Da rest of us 'ave no choice in da matter." He winked.

"I won all me bets." She said to her dad and I thought how quickly her accent had found home.

We said our farewells and Sabrina's dad recommended a place in town to eat and to mention his name.

"Nice family." Bobby said. "I think we better eat there or we'll get another double bogey."

We met the guys at the bar, settled up as I listened to them complain that they had passed up on the best caddy at Ballybunion. Her dad, Scott, had given us a great place to eat and he was so right. He was at the bar when we came in. Either we were at the bar at Ballybunion longer than it seemed or Scott runs as fast as his daughter.

"It's probably his twin brother that owns the place."

Well it was Scott himself. The food was delicious from the Irish stew to the lamb shanks and the beer of course. The eight of us took up a third of the restaurant and half the liquor. When we were done the bus driver walked us straight to the bus. Well he walked straight.

*** Oh you'd make a fine Irishman with that walk; you look like a yokel. ***

Tralee

While we were at Ballybunion two helicopters flew overhead and landed. They told me it was Wayne Huizenga and his buddies. We would see these 'choppers' here and there. It seemed they were following us but that's like some kind of paranoia. Anyway, it was too early to figure out why this might be important to us.

I made sure I selected my caddy before I went to the 'gents'. Pretty stupid considering I did so well the day before by waiting. Beautiful blue skies, green grass with a bit of wind; either it's raining to beat the band or the wind will knock you down. These are the choices in Ireland; pick one.

The terrain looks a bit like New Hampshire but the people here have ages of experience passed down through many generations. There are certain days when even the Irish won't play and, the final proof of their wisdom; they don't even try to make pizza. So there you have it.

Tralee is a traditional Irish form of torture with its rolling hills to hide the greens until the last minute. Trouble left and disaster right but if you're in the right group, life and golf is beautiful.

Four of us formed a perfect group guaranteed to have fun and a game. But I was not in that group. Paul and I were stuck with the other two last minute entries: Steve this-affects-me-how Madeoff and Al. Al is about 6 feet tall. He is not fat; but he is broader at the hips than at the shoulders. Doctor Al Fupdock had dark features complimented by a full head of jet-black hair. I nicknamed him All-fupped-duck., Fupped-duck or just Fup for short. This was perfect because he waddled when he walked, hooks the ball AND… he's a shrink. He does have one psychiatrist's tick; he repeats what you say.

"My dad was a bit of an alcoholic."

"So your dad was an alcoholic, you say…"

You know, that annoying psychiatrist shit. Well Fup does it constantly. He can't help himself. He even annoyed Steve.

Steve Madeoff did not even deserve a nickname. Why waste our time when shithead was perfect. He was some kind of investor/financial/penny-stock/advisor connected to something illegal for sure. I mean he had no ethics on the golf course so this characteristic naturally overflowed into his business dealings.

He was always wheeler-dealing some gig in Canada or a place we could not check on. He seemed to do pretty well. I mean, he had what appeared to be a Rolex Presidential on his wrist. He looked like evil money. I could not figure how he got people to invest when he simply annoyed the ever-lovin' out of everyone, every day.

If I needed a sanity check, Fup was there but I would rather talk to Paul. Paul and I had met at the Lakes club and we ended up doing business together. It was extremely lucrative for my company and his. Our golf games were, well, not so lucrative. We really struggled with this foursome. Even our caddies lost interest. But even the best caddy can't cure a duck hook. I resigned myself to quietly laugh with Paul as the shrink killed a drive to the nether regions barely missing a duck in the pond.

"Hey, Fup, you almost killed your cousin!" Paul yelled.

The shrink in total control of his emotions yelled back. "Up yours, you bastard."

Aaron, our cardiologist buddy has a Charlie-Sheen-before-the-drugs look about him. He was in the foursome behind us probably laughing at the struggles we painted before him. Aaron picked the best caddy; a lean wiry Irishman with a brogue as thick as his hair; hair that was nearly as red as his nose. If I had Sabrina instructing me the day before, Aaron had Allen.

If you are in a dream foursome with a perfect caddy you need only to pull the club back and fire. If you are in a nightmare foursome with a know nothing caddy, just drink and find other amusements.

Steve and the Shrink are slow. I mean Al can pound the ball with the best of us but he has his routine. He tries to line his feet together even with the ball; he puts his right foot back and then his left foot forward. The fupped-duck is knock-kneed and his legs look like a reverse pair of parentheses. He holds his chin up and bends at the waist and places his club behind the ball and remains frozen in time. How long you ask? By now, even Steve has figured out "how this bothers him".

"Come one already." Steve yelled.

Al stepped away from his ball. "Do you mind if I go through my routine without interrupting me!" He starts another prayer.

I kept looking back at Aaron, Tomas, Bobby and Tim. They were on our ass all day like my dad said about the foursome behind you. Leaning on your golf club with your legs crossed is a sign. Standing there interlocking your fingers behind the back of your head is a message but lying on the ground using your golf bag a as a pillow is more than one can bear. This is a point at which the body language is very clear.

"Al, you're a psychiatrist right?"

"Yes I am a psychiatrist."

"What does that body language tell you?" as I point back to our friends behind us.

"They are relaxed and enjoying the moment. What does their body language tell you?"

"That psychiatry is not an exact science!"

He did not respond. I guess he was still steeped in prayer. As it turned out, despite the constant waiting for us Aaron shot five birdies in the last five holes. I guess he had an enormous amount of time to discuss each shot with his caddy and what club to hit. There only remained a matter of when.

We waited on the 18th for them and watched Aaron sink a 40-footer.

"I guess the wait did not bother you at all." I said.

"I had more time to study here than in Med school."

Aaron won all the money so we took him straight to the bar. We were about to order a second round when our bus driver came in. He told us that we would have to leave extra early for Old Head the next day. Our 20 minute helicopter ride is now a 4 hour bus trip. It seems that some self-righteous rich bastard with more money than consideration had hired our helicopter right out from under us. I guess the pilot figured there was more money in a week with him than in one day with us.

** Shakespeare said, "A Wayne by any other name would still smell." **

"No Jack, Shakespeare said, "A rose by any other name would smell as sweet," and they did not say who it was."

*** Yeah, whatever; a Wayne by any other name still stinks.
***

Nothing Like Old Head

*** Nice title. ***

"Hey, Jack I was merely pointing out its uniqueness."

*** Sure you were, pig? ***

Old Head is one-hundred hard kilometers from our hotel in Killarney. It is at the southern tip of County Cork which is the southern tip of Ireland. The harbor is filled with empty masts of anchored schooners, clapping their lines, begging for a sail to join the race. Those that are in the race are spilling bits of wind out of their sails as they tack their way back home to port. A black and white lighthouse is well-positioned high on the Kinsale bluff. The peninsula cried for a golf course and the Irish obliged with perfection. The wind comes straight up the bluff and is the only fence between you and the 100 foot drop that is straight down. There is one lonely road that takes you in to this beautiful painting.

*** And that same road takes you out. ***

"What are you an attorney?"

*** Just trying to help. ***

Although the hundred clicks equals out to sixty miles our left-handed bus makes the two-hour trip in three. The helicopter would have been nice but there was the advantage of finding a great place to eat right outside the gates of Old Head.

We stepped down off the bus and collected our caddies as we checked in. A caddy is a must here to play well and to stay alive. One small step for man could translate into one giant leap to end your asshole support system.

Our foursome was a mixture of souls. I was with handsome Tim, big Tomas and This-bothers-me-how, Steve. I'd say it was windy but Tim's caddy insisted," Aye 'tis unusually calm today. Ah, but the wind, she will pick up soon. We best be quick."

We all did well downwind but as we turned back into it, we all struggled except Tim. Tim hit one beautiful shot after another. Tomas and I hit into the knee high rough and Steve was in deep. All Tomas and I could do is punch out 90 degrees while Steve and his caddy were still looking.

"I'll drop one here." Steve said.

"Ya' do that and I'll drop yer bag and you can caddy yourself. We play by the rules here."

Steve miraculously found his ball even though his experienced caddy could not. Despite his caddy's instructions, Steve tried to take a line down the fairway. He was shaken and looked like he was trying to lose his

111

ball but then his caddy kept finding it. He took a twelve on the hole. That's pretty hard to do without losing a ball but he took a snowman to reach the green and topped it nicely with a snappy four-putt. Tomas and I took a double and Tim managed to par the hole. When Tim had taken his place on the tee he cranked a beauty and made a birdie. Sean said, "I got me the bag of quite the gofer!"

On the very next hole Tim hit a ball slightly off the fairway, maybe ten yards. There was not a stone, nor a gulley, nor a tree to mark its exit. Tim turned to Sean and this was the first I heard of this exchange.

"Do you think we'll find it?" Tim begged.

"Aye." Sean said but then in contradiction he added, "Ya' could wrap bacon 'round it and Lassie couldn't find it."

Since it was the first time we heard the quip; it was hysterical. Even Tim had to laugh at his own misfortune and Sean's spin on it. Tim hit a provisional and we went on. That was about ten years ago and I have heard the story told by other 'inventors'. Not sure if Sean was the originator but it doesn't matter; it is a perfect illustration of colorful Irish humor.

I made a mistake of sorts; a few actually. The first one was that I taught Steve how to plumb-bob on the practice green. Later on the back nine we were on a green on the crest of the bluff when I made, what some might call, the ultimate blunder. Steve was holding his putter shaft up with one eye closed. He held it close to negate the wind. Then he stepped back to get a better look and then took another as I grabbed him before he went off the cliff. We both fell, I backward and Steve on his knees. Steve was so grateful he got up and said, "What! Are you trying to kill me?!!"

*** And this would bother us how? ***

Steve did not go anywhere near the edge for the rest of the day. Tim finished with a miraculous 79 as the rest of us struggled to make bogey golf. Steve shot 112 as he had to stop after nine to buy more balls.

We were thirsty and hit the bar while the caddies cleaned our clubs. We settled up with them and bought a few memories in the clubhouse. I bought Steve a postcard of the bluff and he finally nodded and said, "Thanks."

We were so hungry we hit the first eatery outside the gates of Old Head. We each had something different from smoked salmon to Irish stew, steak and mashed to the fresh catch. There is some misinformation out there that the food in Ireland is not good. We beg to differ; the food is of great quality, finely cooked, delicious and very filling. "Wouldn't you say Jack?"

*** Oh very nice! Hey, why don't you take a walk with me to the bluff; I want to take a few pictures. ***

Patty drove us back to the hotel on the wrong side of the road.

*** They hate that by the way. ***

As Patty drove the conversations got fewer as the snores got louder. When we got to the hotel it was still early evening but we all hit the hay totally exhausted.

*** I guess I'll go have a few drinks with Patty, then. ***

Lahinch

The PGA Pro, Ken Venturi once said "Lahinch is my favorite place outside the USA." He must have been there on a different day than we were. Don't get me wrong I am sure it is beautiful. It was just too windy to open my eyes.

This was our last golf day and we had an unusual afternoon tee time. It was so windy the cows huddled behind each other vying not to be first. They kept tilting their heads trying to find a position where they didn't whistle as much. The bus took a left turn into that wind and I thought we stopped, "I could walk faster than this."

We got to the course and it felt colder than the season would permit. I had a hat but I mistakenly looked up and it went flying to the hotel without me. There was something else missing besides my hat. The place was too empty. Where is the starter? Where are the usual hungry caddies? They always gathered around when new golfers showed but not a soul was outside except us.

"Paul, where are all the caddies?"

"Aye." Patty said as he came out of the pro shop. "Dey went home fir da dee."

"The weather is so bad today they felt there was no work. We'll have to carry our own bags but they'll lend us hand carts." Paul reaffirmed his news. "We'll have no caddies today."

We had spent a week with the shrink. Unlike the Parrot he did not repeat everything he said but he did repeat everything you said.

So Fup repeated, "You mean we have no caddies?"

This was really getting annoying; as we huddled together I heard Steve mock Fup, "That's right Al, we have no caddies, we have no caddies, and we have no caddies!"

The Fupped Duck was fuming.

"Who said that? Tomas? No! It wasn't you! Who said that? Steve that was you! You said that?!!"

The Fup held a club up and added, "I'm going to take this f**king three-iron and I'm going to stick it up your f**king ass until it comes out your f**king throat!"

"And that, my friends, is our psychiatrist." Paul pointed out as Steve ran for cover.

Bobby, the only smart one in our group, decided he'd rather wait for us in the bar. I could not tell you much about Lahinch. I spent most of my time dragging my clubs, looking at the ground or wiping the windblown tears from my eyes. In the other direction the wind caught my bag and handcart and dragged me down the fairway like an uncooperative kid behind his mother. I was in search of a 200 yard nine-iron that I just hit. This is ridiculous. I thought I saw a house with Dorothy and Toto go by. Maybe I should have bought a pair of red spikes.

I chipped one ball up on the green; it hit the pin, fell to the side and then accelerated off the green, down the hill. I could not find it. I grabbed my stuff and said, "That's it. I'm done. I'm joining Bobby in the bar."

That was the day I quit.

*** Yeah, well I'm not falling for that one. ***

Home sweet home

All good trips have to end and so did this one. Before we left we had one more round but if you ever go to Ireland and you do not bring back some Irish linen for the ladies well, how's single life treating you?

The night after we ordered dinner Tim and I ran downstairs for a smoke. Tim was single and so when a few young ladies went by he felt obliged to say something.

"Are you girls from around here?"

They giggled and said yes.

Tim said, "Then could you give me directions to your house?"

And they laughed, giggled and gave Tim their address. You see the difference between sexual harassment and gentlemanly behavior is more about how good looing a guy is than what he says. Tim looked a bit like Tom Hanks; a taller thinner, in shape Tom Hanks. The girls could not resist him. So when we went shopping for the girls the next day Tim did not really have a commitment to buy anything. We all split up on Main Street in Killarney to try a few stores.

I went into this Irish Linen store which was run by what had to be Miss Ireland. Her name was Courtney and I thought this would be a good time to pull a joke on Tim. So I took Courtney aside and explained how the trick would work and she laughed and said, "Aye, that sounds like fun." I think she said "foon" but I got the drift.

So Tim finally comes to the store, Courtney looked over at me and I nodded. She casually walked around the aisles and when she got to Tim she said. "Yes, I do live around here and I'll give you directions to my house."

I said, "That's not exactly what we planned."

"I know; I know." She said. "I got nehr-voos so I improvised."

** Funny she wasn't nervous when you were talking to her. **

117

I got some linen things for my wife and my mother-in-law and was the first one to the bar next door. You can always find a bar in Ireland. If you're in a shop the bar is next door; if you're already in a bar the next one is two-doors down. Sometimes the store in between is a liquor store. If I am exaggerating than it is just an Irish thing and you can ignore me for saying so.

The place was almost empty except for two lads; one of them did not have his face on the bar. I said good day to the upright lad and was glad to find that he was the bartender.

And I said with my best brogue, "Good day to ya' lads; I'll have a pint, if ya' please."

"Aye, so yer from the states, the first one's on us then." He said. And when the other guys drifted in the third, the fifth and every other drink was free… did I mention that we never did get to play golf that day. We drank until dinner, fell down, had dinner, drank, fell down and dragged ourselves around town like locals. And then and only then no one questioned our brogue or figured us to be from the States. The very next morning we went to the airport; a miserable experience is a long trip with a hangover. Tomas prescribed some hair of the dog and that worked. I'm not sure why but it always does for little while anyway.

** I know why. You just had too much blood in your alcohol stream. **

5: Just Desserts

If a baseball umpire called me safe when I was out, I would get up, dust my pants off and keep my mouth shut. The same goes for many sports, especially hockey, football and basketball where players seem to go out of their way to cheat. Elbows flying and cheap jabs are part of the game. Your team expects you to behave in this manner even though God sees everything. You might say that God knows that this is part of the game. But what about the umpire or a referee that cheats? That must never be allowed in any sport. No way, they'd hang him. Look at South America; a cheating soccer referee would never make it out of the arena.

In golf you must call yourself out or safe. This is the code, the rock that makes golf not just a game, but the very soul and character of the man or woman who plays it. It defines you. Let's face facts, in golf you are the referee, the umpire, and the judge. Some guys hold to the USGA rules tighter than a Long Island girl to her virginity; that is, everyone "claims" to follow the rules.

Some rules, it seems, are like white lies. It is blatantly wrong to give the wrong handicap but it seems okay for some to pad it. Don pointed out that a few tricky-dicks have what he called "a well-managed handicap". They know when they have cheated and believe me, so do we. And we've all witnessed the guy who tees off with a Titleist and holes out with a Top Flite. These are not only stories. They are based on fact and your head may nod as your recall similar events and characters. For some these will be stories of wrong-doing; for others these will be pointers to be logged for later use, I'm afraid. This is a great time for a highlighter.

The 365 Day Loser

Charlton is a pretentious name for a mother to give a son so, to stop the teasing, he called himself Chuck. When you are a cheater the last thing you want is to call attention to yourself. It did not matter; we called him "Snakes". Snakes had one of those well-managed handicaps Don had mentioned along with some well-concealed intelligence. He had all of the tricks that one man could have and, when he did not, he could make one up on the fly. He is dark-haired and looked like Gomez (John Astin) but is as tall as Lurch; the Addam's family resemblance was remarkable.

We played a tricky golf course with a lot of blind shots in the Jewish Alps of upstate New York. These are the Catskills and we were playing at Grossinger's. Snakes had already twice hit into Don's group and he had been warned as many times to wait. Artie was about to hit his approach shot when a ball came bouncing by at a good clip.

"I wonder who that could be." Don said.

Artie snapped his wallet out like a gunslinger, "I bet 5 bucks it's Chuck!"

"I'll take half of that?" I said.

** Cheap bastard. **

Don snapped around as he thought he heard something; after coming up empty he repeated Jack's comment, "Cheap bastard."

Sure enough when the ball stopped it was identified as the Snakes' ball. Artie holstered his wallet, took his stance and hit the green with his shot. It spun back and rolled down the hill off the green. We all missed the green left, short or right so we blamed it on Snakes' ball. Not to mention this is strike three for hitting into us. Chuck's ball was served a lesson; it was quickly picked up and put into someone's pocket.

This may seem a little extreme but you don't know Snakes. Even felons can't expect amnesty after three convictions. We headed up to the green. Snakes never came up to apologize; he did not come up and ask if we had seen his ball. Nothing!

** He'll slither out a solution, I'm sure. **

We finished the round and went back to the hotel to check in, shower and meet for dinner. We had barely sat down at our big table when Snakes busted in with his well-rehearsed story.

"I was on the fifteenth when I crushed this drive over the hill down the middle but when I got over the hill my ball was nowhere in sight. We all looked; we looked everywhere and I was almost out of time. I took one last look down the line from the tee and kept walking across the fairway and there it was. It was nestled in the hole against the 150 yard marker! I must have hit it even further than I thought. I took the free drop, of course. ..." He tried to continue but got interrupted.

"You mean this ball right here?" Don pointed to the table and there was a ball in front of him with Snakes' markings.

If Snakes was honest he would have gone back to the tee and hit a provisional. Had he rode up to the green and apologized he may have gotten his ball back. Either of these honest choices would have given Don a chance to give him a break. The Snake was completely busted and all of our suspicions about him had come to light in front of our world. He never even questioned Don on why he picked up his ball.

But then Chuck tried one more plea bargain, "Oh? Maybe the one I found was my ball from last year."

*** Funny he never questioned how the ball got to the table. ***

Closest to the "Pen"

Two days later we were still in the mountains of upstate NY playing at the Concord. Don was ahead of us. Chuck was in my group and he made sure Don was long gone before he hit. After a few holes we got to our first par three.

"Holy Crap. This is a long one; it's 210 yards. Some of the guys will have trouble getting a driver there." I pointed to the scorecard. We have a very mixed group in age and some of our guys are in their eighties.

"It's not as bad as it looks. It is downhill but you're right, I doubt the Parrot will get it there." Artie agreed.

"He should consider giving up the game." Chuck came out of his worm hole and gave us his typical sympathetic wisdom.

"He really is a snake, isn't he?" Artie said to me. I nodded. It really was rhetorical but out of the woods a tree creaked.

** More than you know. **

Artie looked over his shoulder and seeing no one there he grabbed two beers from the cooler.

"Ready?"

"Always", as I accepted this beautiful ice cold Bud in a can and leaned back.

We popped the tops and Artie identified the popping sound, "Irish crickets."

Our men's club has a closest to the pin on each par three. There's some money involved and Snakes hit his shot on the green while the rest of us chose our own private bunkers. Chuck was still about twenty five feet away. Don leaves a business card at each par 3 with a tee shoved through it. Chuck did the routine. He picked up the card, flipped it over, scrolled his name on the back and stuck them into the green next to his ball. Snakes fixed his ball mark and a few others. This would be both notable and honorable but he did this because they were in the line of his putt. He slithered back to his ball.

We were only the second group but the last group would pick up the cards and the money would be doled out accordingly. We all got up and down and Snakes two-putted. We were a quick foursome. The group behind us was nowhere in sight. So once again we were off to the next hole at a quick pace. We circled around a hill to the next tee box and were about to walk up with our drivers when Chuck held up.

"Ah shit, I must have dropped my glove back there. I'll be right back." Chuck hopped in the cart and drove away alone.

** *His glove is in his pocket.* ** Jack whispered.

"Hmm? Be right back. Gotta pee." I told the guys.

I climbed the hill to where I could see the previous green. I had some bushes as cover. I saw Chuck jump out of the cart, run across the green and move his mark to within 9 feet. He took the glove from his pocket and jumped in his cart and took off. I ran down the hill took his mark and put it 45 feet away and returned over the hill to the tee box. Chuck beat me back of course.

"I had to take a leak." I was a bit winded but managed to ask, "Did you find your glove."

"Yeah, it was right where I left it." Chuck said.

** Thanks, Yogi. **

"Right were you left it? Gee thanks for that one Yogi." I repeated as we laughed.

** Hey, you stole my line. **

"Sorry. "

** It's not like you can give me any credit. **

Well as it turned out a few foursomes later the Parrot did use his driver and knocked it to about 25 feet or so. He four-putted but took the closest to the pin. When we got in Chuck could not believe this old man had beaten him.

"How close where you?" Chuck inquired.

"I was about twenty-five, twenty five feet; way inside, way inside yours."

Don handed the Parrot his ten bucks while the Snake remained coiled in painful silence. After all, what could he say?

** Sweet!!! **

There's a Hole in My Pocket

The club only traveled twice a year, once in the spring and once in the fall. Saturday's we played at the club and Ted was in charge. On Thursday's Don had sole possession of the club's helm and would find a course closer to his house than the rest of us. This way we could pick him up on the way.

We were out on this new course called National on Long Island; not the ritzy expensive one you're thinking of; the other one. It used to be an old sod farm which means it is lush, fertile and perfect to grow all sorts of shit to prevent you from reaching your goal. They did a great job. It had been too flat so they brought in some bulldozers to make real hills. The Caterpillar boys sat on possessed over-zealous machines that took the once flat land and undulated the bejesus out of it. Now you get one peek at the fairway either from the tee box or on your second shot, but not both. Since it was once a sod farm, the fairways and the first cut are plush and green. There is no second cut; it is actually what you might call *never cut* and it is tannish-brown like fields of wheat. If you hit your ball in the wheat you might end up on the news or on a milk carton. You'd be lucky to find the ball at all. You might find three others but none would be yours. Luck, you see, comes in many forms; Jack believes in luck fervently.

** Luck? Sure, you're either born under a bad sign, or you have no luck at all. **

"You're kind of a glass is half empty guy, aren't you?"

** No, I'm a kind of an empty-all-of-your-hopes kind of guy. **

Speaking of luck, I drew the Grossinger Snake as my opponent.

It is a sad thing to find that you have a hole in your pocket. You could lose your favorite marker, a few tees or even worse your money or your wallet. This is all possible, that is, if the hole is at the bottom of your pocket. When I went to grammar school the teachers would put a golf ball down your pants. If the ball did not hit the floor, your pants were too tight and you'd be taking a note home to your parents. If the hole is high enough in the pocket, small but as big as it needs to be, you can squeeze a ball down your pant leg. If this happens on the golf course you're a damned cheatin' bastard. I don't have any other way to explain this incident so I am going with long pants and a 'high hole in the pocket' to explain this one.

It was one of those gorgeous days on Long Island in October that we call Indian summer. It is cool in the morning like fall but warm in this casual afternoon as there is no-jacket-required. I smiled at this perfectly unspoiled day until the guys reminded me to "keep an eye on him" as we headed for the first tee.

The Snake managed to play pretty decent on the first 3 holes, honestly making a par on each one. He had hit each fairway, had a good lie, hit the green or near enough to 2 putt his way to even par. I was one over so I am already one down.

When we got to the fourth the wind was at us. It is a par five and you could lay-up or try to carry a gulley of wheat, stone, poison ivy, briars and miscellaneous barbed wire running across the fairway. Launching your driver over something like this is called "carrying the shit". You can't see the fairway on the other side so you have to gauge your success on how well you hit it. Snakes was feeling pretty cocky about now and he started getting lofty goals.

Snakes pulled out his drive as he bragged, "I did not come here to lay-up!" I could hear a cold snicker of a breeze coming toward us from the waves of grain; it sounded very much like you know who.

** Ah, yes, my favorite, lofty goals made of false hopes. **

Snakes pulled back his driver slowly but overanxious to hit the shot (before Jack or the devil could see him); he released too early. He had knocked it over the hill but far right into the amber waves of grain. To finish the song, His Majesty, Snakes, turned as purple as the mountains.

"God damn it!!" He screamed and then figuring to pick a pocket or two, he recovered his words, "It'll probably be okay though; I'm past the shit."

"Not in this wind." Jimmy said and we all agreed.

"I really hit that one good." Snakes added.

"You sure did; right down the Rush Limbaugh highway."

"I like Rush." Chuck said.

** Then he'll enjoy the lie. ** Jack said.

"I'm not so inclined. I follow only one party; the Cocktail Party." I suggested. "You can keep the rest."

After a bit of a protest, Snakes finally laid up with a provisional. The rest of us hit irons before the shit because, unlike Snakes, we came here to lay-up. After we hit our second shots over never-never land we drove around and down to the right to find Snake's first ball. This was nearly impossible. You would have to step on the ball if you had any hopes of finding it. Snakes was already looking in an area that Tiger Woods couldn't reach from the tee.

Suddenly Snakes yelled out, "found it!"

"Really!?"

"Yep, it's my Precept and it's got my 'J' right on it."

Almost as this left his lips, Jim yelled, "Over here! I got your ball over here." Jim was about 50 yards short of Snake's find.

"It's your Precept with your little 'J' on it.

Jim was the oldest in the group being in his mid-seventies. A big solid man in great shape; even his hair refused to turn gray. Jim plays the ball down and has no tolerance for the likes of cheaters. The Snake was nailed again but he rifled off an excuse, "I must have dropped that one while I was looking."

Jim said, 'You were never anywhere near here."

"No I meant I must have dropped *this* one while I was looking. It must have fallen out of my pocket."

I was shaking my head at two things: How does he come up with this stuff so fast and why does he think any of us believe him. Snakes walked over to Jim.

"It is really an awful lie." Jim dealt out some justice.

"You can say that again." I said.

"How do you know, from all the way over there?" Snakes asked.

"If you use your ears you can tell an awful lie from quite a distance?" I said.

Jim, Joe and I watched in snickering silence with Jack as Snakes tried to hack away and finally got it to the fairway.

"Just so we're clear, you're laying four already." Jim said as we all nodded.

"I know, I know. I wish I'd never found the damned thing!"

Nursery rhymes are often spawned from real events and I could hear Jack as he started singing in the breeze.

** *There's a hole in your pocket, dear liar, dear liar.* **

A Bad Penny

I don't know why I am amazed. But after someone has just been caught you would think their best behavior would be in order; at least for a while. Well that lasted about one hole.

On the 6th, par 3, we finally had some trees to contend with. Joe hit a good shot but one of the limbs knocked it into the front bunker. Snakes and I hit our tees shots on the green. Like Jim, Joe refused to let his hair turn gray but Joe's aged knees were giving him trouble. It took him time to climb down into the trap. He asked Snakes if he could mark his ball and Snakes put a penny down. Joe hit a pretty decent bunker shot that passed Snake's mark, 3 feet closer to the hole. Snakes marked Joe's ball with another penny. Jim went down to help Joe rake the bunker; I handed Jim the rake as I helped Joe up and we all walked to the green.

"This one is yours, Joe." Snakes points to the one further way.

"Ah, no, no, no, Snakes; that one is yours, you're away."

"Are you sure?"

"I'm positive. Remember he hit his bunker shot right over your mark?"

"Oh, yeah, you may be right about that. Okay, Joe you want to move your mark or putt out?"

"No, no, no…I want *you* to show *me* the line." Joe protested.

Snakes took his gray metal putter in hand and swung a few practice putts. He left his putt about two-feet short. He walked over, nonchalantly hit it and missed. He turned to us and said, "That was good, I was just in a hurry because I've got to pee." and trotted off the green into the woods.

I yelled after him, "How about I take a leak at your house, miss the bowl and say, 'that was good I was just in a hurry cause I had to putt."

I made par and Joe made his sandy. Jim had made a 4 and said so. As we walked off a slight breeze came from the trees and it sounded like they whispered,

** *Cheatin' bastard.* **

I don't know how long he had been using that putter but something in my mind was stirring. It did not occur to me until we gave Snakes a 14 inch putt. I did not realize that he was that close or I would have hit it back to him after his chip shot. I had had my own troubles in the bunker. So, taking our gift, he walked over and without bending over he picked up his marker with the back of his putter. There was something about that move that was unsettling. I watched him closer over the next few holes.

Then on the ninth hole it struck me; sometimes he marks with a penny and other times he has this gray metal marker like the one he scooped up on the gimme. I had gone over the green and had to chip back over a hill. I walked from the hole to see what I had and had to ask Snakes to mark his ball. He took out the gray marker. I nearly holed out and Snakes had to give me the putt. As I walked over to pick it up. I stopped at Snake's marker as if I did not want to step in his line. I paced off fifteen feet. What I did not tell anyone was that I paced of 21 feet before I took my chip shot. Snakes had moved his marker 6 feet closer and I figured out how he did it.

"What kind of marker is that Snakes?"

"It is an old 1943 steel penny; they stopped using copper during World War two. If you find a copper 1943 they are worth a ton of money; this one isn't worth more than a nickel or two."

"I notice you don't use it all the time." wanting him to notice my careful observation.

"It's my lucky penny so I use it when I need some luck."

"A mark like that sometimes makes a putt seem a lot shorter, doesn't it?" as I stared a hole right through him.

That marker never left his pocket the rest of the round and I said to the trees, "You ain't shittin' me Jack; cheatin' bastard, indeed!"

*** And everyone knows it. ***

By the time we got to the 18th I had had about all of Snakes that one man can stand. It's hard enough to pay attention to your own game without babysitting a Slick Willy. He'd hit a ball in the rough and I found it. I wanted to step on it and ground it into the earth to be found by an archaeologist to be named later. I wussed out.

"Over here, Snakes." I yelled to him. He was forty yards ahead of me, hoping to drop one from his pocket. I said as I looked to the sky I heard a whisper.

** The man has no shame. **

His ball was deep enough in the rough that you had to be right on top of it to see it. I waited until he got there and walked to the middle of the fairway to my ball. I turned to see if I was away and I could see Snakes on the side. That's not surprising as Snakes is over six feet tall. What was surprising was that now, NOW, I can see his ball from the fairway.

"You're away right?" he said as I caught sight of him and his Precept.

I yelled, "Yes." I was but I had a nine iron in my hand and I was going to hit him with it.

I marched briskly across the fairway as he said, "That's okay. Ready golf; I'll hit." But I was already on him as I stuck my nine-iron between his legs.

"That ball is on a freaking tee!" I screamed at him with all that is holy and all that is not!!

Snakes simply looked at me matter-of-factly and said, "Yeah, you're right. What are the odds of that happening?"

I knocked it off the tee, "That's a two stroke penalty for moving the ball."

"But I didn't…"

"Don't even…I'll let the guys decide." But the guys were already there.

"Hey what's with the tee?" Jim asked.

"Fine I'll take the two strokes." Snakes resigned.

"And an automatic loss of hole in our match you cheating bastard." I thought Jim was going to pound him into the ground.

The Snake was busted once again and he lost the hole and the match because of it. Then again, I wonder how many things we did not catch him at during the match. Anyway, that day proved something to me: that there is a God and that I know that he is not Jack, but I think Jack might have His ear.

"Save me a seat will ya', Jack?"

** I'll save you a seat but I'm not saying where. **

NCIS[2] Rules of Golf

Even the rules of golf can play the most rotten of tricks. As in all such rules this is very tricky so please stay with me on this.

In four ball match play, Artie and opponent Snakes, each hit a drive left over the hill. Artie is usually longer than Snakes so when they come over the top they see the first ball at the edge of the fairway. They proceed to look for Artie's ball.

The Snake says, "Well, I'll go hit so we don't hold up play."

---

[2] NCIS (September 2003 to present) is a CBS television series, revolving around a fictional team of special agents from the Naval Criminal Investigative Service, The show was created by Donald Bellisario, Don McGill.

Snakes hits his shot deep into the water. Suddenly Artie finds a ball but it is not his; it is actually Snakes' ball!

The ball that Snakes *mistakenly* hit was actually Artie's ball. Since Snakes hit the wrong ball in match play he is out of the hole. Since no one actually identified the ball that went into the water, Artie's ball is deemed lost under Rule 27-1c. Artie must suffer a stroke and distance penalty. He must go back and hit again from the tee. Effectively that leaves their respective partners to duel it out.

Now let's say Snakes knew that Artie was favored to win the hole and there is a strong possibility that the Snake did this on purpose. What if this was found to be true?

*** Artie should be entitled to take relief by removing one of Snakes' testicles to finish the hole; under Gibbs' Rule 27-1c-snip[3] ****

The Rules Guy

The rules of golf are tricky. They were most likely written by the same people who wrote the U.S. Federal Tax Code. Over the years I have tried my best to

---

[3] Special Agent Leroy Jethro Gibbs is a character from the TV show, NCIS. He makes up humorous yet sensible rules to be followed and assigns a number to each one.

understand them but they are fogged by some of the USGA decisions which render logic a useless tool.

A lot of people on the golf course just want to play the game. There are others who profess to know some of the rules like those people in Washington. That does not stop them from officiating on your predicament on the course. I completely understand the old western sentiment of hanging a horse thief. A few times I've had the distinct displeasure of some asshole that misquotes a rule in my disfavor to his total satisfaction. There is something radically wrong with a human who wallows in your misery; to invent that misery requires the ultimate punishment. It is during these occasions that I look for a nice solid oak with just the right limb and a strong rope.

Maybe I am over generous to my competition. I was in a match play event at the club and my fellow competitor, Mark Sellers, had asked me for a ruling.

"Can I place my club in the hazard so I can take my stance without slipping into the water?"

"Sure as long as you don't move anything or test the condition. Go ahead."

I think most of us try to be obliging within the rules. On the very next hole I hit a high 8 iron before the green. It should have been an easy par from there but when I got to my ball it was hanging half out of its own pitch mark with a big hunk of mud on the back.

"Can I get relief? I want to take a drop under the imbedded ball rule."

139

"Well your ball is not totally in the pitch mark. It's mostly out of it. According to the rules, if it is not in the pitch mark it must be played as it lies."

"It's partially in the pitch mark!"

"Rule 25-2 states that you get relief if, I say again IF it is in its own pitch mark. Your ball is not entirely in the pitch mark. So you do not get relief." Mark stated emphatically.

"But it is touching the pitch mark and nearly impossible to play. "

"Well the rules are not kind sometimes and you are more than halfway out."

"Fine, I'll play like it is."

Not only do I have to hit this ball over my pitch mark, I can't putt it and I can't clean the hunk of mud attached to the back of the ball. I tried to blade putt it but it hopped and went nowhere. I was still twenty feet from the hole. Mark made par and I two putted and lost the hole.

The match went back and forth and we ended up in a tie. When I got in I asked the head pro for the rule book and explained my situation.

"Who gave you that ruling?" Bryan was annoyed.

"Mark."

"Well that is totally the wrong answer. Any ball touching its own pitch mark is considered in the pitch mark. Like any ball touching the green is on the green." And Bryan showed me the ruling.

"Unfortunately, Mr. Martin, I am sorry but the match has to stand as a tie. You will need to play a sudden tie-breaker."

Bryan called Mark to the first tee. When Mark got there Bryan asked Mark what happened on the third hole.

"Wayne wanted relief but his ball was outside the pitch mark."

"Was it touching the pitch mark?"

"Well I don't remember now but he did not get relief."

"I see." said Bryan. "I think I'll join you guys for the rest of the match."

Mark and I tied the first hole but on the second Mark hit his second shot over the green. There's a bank that goes down to the water there. While I was preparing for my second shot, Mark was in his golf cart heading to the back of the green before Bryan and I could get there. I had hit my ball short left and it fell just barely in the water.

"I'm still up!" he shouted.

Bryan looked at me then bent his head down and shook it back and forth.

"Where's the closest oak tree?" I said

** *I'll get the rope.* ** Jack added.

Behind that green a severe banks slopes down to the water. A ball coming to rest at that speed on that bank would have to fall in. But Mark quickly chipped up as we got there and his ball came to rest right next to the hole. I was in trouble. His par was imminent. Half my ball was out of the water.

"I should be able to hit it." I was desperate.

I took my shoes off and started down the bank. It was slippery. Mark marked his ball and hustled over to watch.

"Careful! I would not touch the hazard with that club." Mark said.

Bryan interrupted, "Sorry, Mr. Sellers that constitutes advice. The penalty for advice in match play is loss of hole. According to the rules you lose the hole and therefore the match goes to Mr. Martin."

"That's not fair!" Mark complained.

Bryan said, "Well the rules are not kind sometimes. Congratulations, Mr. Martin."

"Thanks Bryan."

Mark stormed off to his cart without a handshake and without as much as a goodbye.

*** Sometimes life's a pitch mark and sometimes it's a bitch Mark. ***

"Very clever, Jack. Thanks."

*** You're welcome! ***

There is a God

My buddy Jay and I were playing for the South Florida Golf Association. We had white golf shirts that said so and blue shorts. This sounds very exclusive but it was only a bunch of guys from the Fort Lauderdale area. On this one given Sunday we were playing against another club of southern hobos from the Country Club of Miami. People often joke that the reason Miami is great is because it is so close to the United States. They do not lie. There are signs in Spanish everywhere and if you don't speak it you can't even ask for directions. We got to the course late as we missed a few turns. We had no time to warm up. We paid our green fees and made the obligatory three practices putts; just as it was written and so it shall remain..

"Wow, pretty fast."

"They're slow."

We headed to the first tee.

We met Brady and Jose at the first tee. Jose was little guy, with a friendly solid handshake and smiled with the whitest teeth I'd ever seen. He was a gentleman and to no surprise, a dentist. He looked a bit like Cheech Marin and we told him so.

"Yeah, I get that a lot." He laughed. "If I had his money, I'd burn mine."

"I'm a one-handicap so I guess I will be giving everybody strokes." Brady pointed his nose to God.

Brady R. Blasdell III had an engraved golf bag and an air of self-entitlement. His handshake was minimal; as if we were beneath him. No one really cared what he did or didn't do for a living. He looked a little like a young

Robert Wagner but no one wanted to compliment this arrogant son-of-a-bitch.

"Actually, I will be giving you one-stroke." Jay corrected Brady and his nose.

Jay is a zero handicap; *scratch* as they say. Jay is also leaner and taller; Brady tries to walk to get higher ground. Jay has dark hair somewhat covered with a Cincinnati Reds cap. His arms and legs are covered with 50 SPF and he smells like Coppertone. Jay always has a smile like he's about to tell a dirty joke. His friendly ways are in direct contrasts to Brady's.

Brady was obviously not used to being something other than the center of attention. A breeze from the trees was welcome on this hot Florida day and it carried with it a low sound,

** *I don't like this guy.* ** Then there was a slight pause and another breeze,

** *If you beat him; he will leave.* **

I was not sure what that meant exactly but I knew Jack; he would be watching every move. Jay turned around to look for a corn field but there was none.

"Did you hear that?" Jay asked.

"Hear what?"

"Hmmm, never mind, I guess it was only the wind." Jay said as he pulled out his driver.

Brady threw a tee in the air to see who went first. The tee hit the ground pointing at Brady but then it did a bounce-flip and settled right at us. Brady swept up the tee with his premature aggravation; his hand was too quick for his finger and the tee slipped through and hit Jose, his partner.

"Hey!" Jose complained.

"Oh, for God's sake; it's just a tee and you shouldn't have been standing there!" Apparently Brady did not like to lose at anything.

*** You would be wise…*
To keep your eyes
*On the one we despise ****

Jay said, "That breeze sure feels good and…"

"Yeah and I like the sound of it. It seems to be in our favor." I said as I looked to the trees and I whispered, "Poetry Jack, really… poetry?"

*** Why not? ****

I was still taking a few swings to warm up by the trees and I asked Jay if he would mind going first.

"No Problem."

Jay stripped the head-cover off his driver and tossed it toward the cart as he teed the ball. It seemed all of this was in one smooth motion. He held the shaft upright and looked at the head of his driver for a moment and lowered it like Jack's poetry but smoother.

*** I heard that! ****"

Jay set his feet and frame to his comfort and effortlessly took the club back and through as he ripped a long drive right down the middle of the fairway. Jay did not look up. He picked up the tee, retrieved his head cover and graciously accepted our compliments.

"Thanks guys."

I tried to imitate Jay's exact motions as near as I could; I even hit a slight draw as Jay had done. It was right down the middle but not as far. I took a compliment from Jay and Jose but Brady did not say a word, so the breeze added a comment,

** *Asshole.* **

"Thanks Jose; thanks Jay." I purposely left out Brady and nodded my agreement to the trees and Jack.

Brady and I had had no contact except that first poor handshake. I did not like him and I don't usually judge so quickly.

The first up on their side was Jose; he was a twelve handicap and hit a mildly safe shot down the left. Jose is older than the rest of us. His swing lacked any shoulder power and he was 30 yards behind me.

We all said good shot; well most of us; Brady was silent. I got the feeling that Jose liked Brady less than we did. Brady took some high velocity practice swings and held a smooth finish for the cameras. You can tell by his face as his lips lost color and tightly disappeared that he was going to rip the ever-loving out of his tee ball. His entire body was possessed by the illusion that he would hit his ball past Jay's.

He took the club back long and low as his back was toward the fairway but he did not finish and fired violently blocking the ball into the woods toward the out of bounds.

"That might be out of bounds." his partner noted, "You might want to hit a provisional."

Jay looked at me and said, 'Yeah, it looked to me like it went OB."

** That is definitely out of bounds! **

Brady looked around as if he had heard Jack as well. "Okay, provisional, but I think the first one stayed in."

"I am pretty sure that went into the parking lot." I added, "But you never know, an old lady may have taken a beaner and soccer-headed it back into play."

Brady leered at me as if he could burn a hole. I just smiled and shrugged. You could tell that we had a firm agreement to hate each other's guts. He hit his provisional into the trees again but not as bad. I swore that he was aiming that way on purpose. We started looking for both balls. Brady was so far back but insisted on looking 30 yards ahead of where he went in. I found a ball right where I thought his provisional might be.

"Here it is." I yelled

Brady walked over, looked down and said with no hesitation, "This is my first one."

It was still in terrible position and he would be of no help to his partner. Jay and I let it slide but it was an unnerving intro into what lay ahead. Brady attempted a miracle shot and as with all miracles they should be left to a higher authority. Brady hit a tree; it hit him and then bounced out of bounds.

"Ouch! Damn it!"

"There IS a God." I blurted out loud.

Jay had had enough of this asshole too and let him have it, "Let's see, two strokes for your ball hitting you, plus you're out of bounds, AGAIN! So you can take a drop. You will be hitting your sixth shot or should it be your eighth!?"

Jay and I spent the day both *hovering over* and *laughing at* Brady's misfortunes and correcting his math. He was forced to play honest golf to a handicap he could never cover. His partner, Jose, was a great guy and we all had beers afterwards, without Brady. Brady threw his clubs in the car and left the golf cart in the parking lot for someone less entitled to take back. Jose explained that no one wanted to be Brady's partner but it was his turn.

"That may be the most despicable guy I have ever played with." I said.

"You didn't exactly hide your feelings. You rode him all day like a rented mule." Jay smiled.

"I wasn't alone."

Jose explained, "I walked with a hand cart because I didn't want to even ride with the bastard."

We made some plans to play with Jose and a different fourth guy for the following week. The experience was so different and Jose had the round of his life. We all played better and even when we didn't, it simply did not matter. We were relaxed. Golf tugs at your heart and pulls at your very soul. The greatest gift is the company and the people you meet when you play this game as it should be played. Golf is a single lane highway that moves only as fast as the slowest group. There are some people who are a pleasure to be with, even if you are stuck in traffic.

** And then again there are those that you'd like to stop and throw off the bridge. **

You Don't Know Nothin'

"Hi, Grandma."

"Hi dear, how are you? How's Stephie?"

My wife does not like that nickname but she did not want to hurt Grandma's feelings. But don't try it yourself, you are no Grandma Lenny.

"Steph is fine. How are you? How's Grandpa?"

"Just fine, dear, hold on, I'll get him."

I met my wife's grandfather a year before I married their granddaughter. Grandpa played golf and we hit it off right from the very first day we met.

I could hear him in the background as he made his way to the phone. "Ah, what do I want to talk to him for?" and then he gets on and says, "Oh hi son, how are you?" and then he'd laugh.

"Great. I wanted to remind you I am bringing my friend Jay tomorrow. What time should we be there?"

"We all get there at 7:00 AM. They'll fit you in with another twosome. I have to play in my usual group tomorrow but I'll be in front or behind you. Can you pick me up around 10 of?"

"Sure Grandpa, see you tomorrow."

"Okay, son."

In his youthful days he had run some numbers for the mob and when the time came and he earned enough, he ran an appliance store in Peekskill, NY. And so it was arranged; he would own it. He had been a boxer and his voice had more gravel than a blue stone driveway. He was closing on eighty years-old. His gray hair and box-like frame were still imposing even though he only topped out at about 5 foot-6 inches. He had a firm, hard handshake and a constant smile. Grandpa Artie had a way about him and everyone he met hoped to be counted as his friend. In his earlier days, Jackie Gleason had gone to Artie's store and they became instant and close friends. If Gleason wanted a pink refrigerator for his pool and he did, Artie had it made for him. Grandpa Artie was the ultimate man's man. You would count yourself blessed for having spent time with him.

By the time I met them, Grandpa Artie and Grandma Lenny had retired to Delray Beach. My wife and I traveled down to see them shortly after we were married. He took me to his men's club to play golf with his buddies. After a few years Stephanie and I moved to Florida not more than 20 miles away. Steph's grandfather was a proud man. Stephanie is nearly 11 years younger and for me to call him "Grandpa", was a mixture of love and pain.

"My granddaughter married this old bastard and now he calls me "Grandpa!"" He gravels loudly and laughs.

They called me 'The Kid". Grandpa called me "son" to ease the pain. All of these fine gentlemen are from the greatest generation the U.S. has ever known, World War II vets. If I had chosen to live in a different lifetime I would have picked that time, that patriotism. Some barely speak of it while others boast that they won the war by themselves. No matter, you can see the pride there and all I can do is admire the time and these men. So if they take a few liberties on the golf course, for them, I say.

"Hey! Sorry, buddy! But the rules are the rules!" I mean there's a dollar on the line.

* Cheap bastard *

"Hi Jack."

* Let them be. *

Jay and I swung by to say hi to Grandma and pick up Grandpa.

"Hi Jay. How's your game?" Grandpa asked. I had forgotten they had met at my house.

"Good days and bad days, Artie. How about you?"

"I wish I had you're game. I wish I had anyone's game." Grandpa said modestly.

We exchanged some golf jokes as we pulled up to the course. The golf clubhouse smelled of sweat, liniment, stale coffee and had walls that cracked from being yelled at. I did not know that yelling had a smell until those days. The room was too small for the purpose, crowed by two folding tables and too many chairs in total disarray. The beaten walls were covered with notices about some tournament and others that had long passed. The only thing new in this room was today's tee sheet and Jay. You had to pay a dollar to cover the only bet and so each veteran would take his turn like this.

"Where's your dollar?"

"It's under your nose you blind bastard!"

"It's on the wrong side, ah, but what do you know?!"

"Ah, you're eyes are fuhkakta. You can't see and you don't know nothin'!"

"Ah, you talk and you talk and you talk but *YOU* don't know nothin'. I'll mark you paid."

"Thank you."

"Ya' velcome, now get lost."

Many were from Brooklyn; some were from Boston and some even admitted they were from New

Hampshire. Throw in some Canadians; guys from Pittsburg and you have a mixture of Jewish, Italian and some Irish all yelling at a volume that had me looking for the door. You see everyone in that room was hard of hearing and very soon that would be me. They had an executive par 64 course they played on designed by Pete Dye himself. Sometimes I would bring a friend along and this time I brought, my scratch golfer buddy, Jay. We sat in the clubhouse for a half an hour before teeing off. Jay was soaking in the bitter camaraderie of the octogenarians as I just shook my head. Here we go again.

"Ah what do you know?" One yelled as he waved a disgusted hand.

"What do YOU know? You don't know nothin'! You talk, and you talk, and you talk, but don't know NOTHIN'!"

Jay was laughing out of control in the corner as I shook my head in embarrassment.

Jay leaned over, "This is great stuff!"

The same argument erupts, "Where's your dollar?"

"Right here you blind bastard!"

"I'll mark you paid, now go away."

Oh I forgot to mention they are apparently playing for the last buck they own. The arguing continues. The room is filled with the din of loud voices and whistling hearing aids. Finally after being tortured with these bad vibrations, Jay and I escape to the practice green. My ears were ringing like I just left a rock concert.

"God, I had to get out of there."

"Ah come on! I was enjoying it. That should be in a movie."

"Yeah well that show would be a repeat for me. I don't know how Grandpa can stand it."

After the first three foursomes took off, Jay and I got hooked with a twosome. Grandpa was in the group ahead of us. They have a ritual of waving the group behind them up. They watch until the last tee shot settles. Then they putt out while the group behind them walks to their ball. In the crowded clubs of New York this wave-up routine is required; it is not an option. Some golfers automatically know that this speeds up play while the math eludes those with lower SAT scores. It is however, not without a certain element of danger. Here we are in sunny Delray Beach, Florida not yet 8:15 AM and the sun is already brutal. Jay has on so much SPF 50 he looks like a Central Park statue.

"You better not stand still too long. A bird might land on you. Although who would notice, they poop white."

"Does the word melanoma mean anything to you?"

"Alright, fine, I'll put some on too." I conceded as we waited by the 1st tee.

It's a 165 yard par three and each perfectly aged World-War II vet lays up using his driver. This is performed like a military march as each group repeats the process. Finally we get our turn at the first tee and the group in front of us is now waving us up. There they are standing in full battle array a mere six inches behind the flag without any vision even close to 20-20; a collective group of four blind mice.

Jay asked, "What on earth are they doing?"

"They are waving us up."

"Yeah but we are going to hit them. They should move to the back. We could yell fore but who would hear us."

"We'll just point, wave and yell."

So I swept a six iron through a Titleist and it dropped right at Grandpa's feet as we pointed, yelled and waved. He was so proud of me when I got there he said, "That's it! You're out of the will!"

I think it's a Jewish thing. I mean who thinks in terms of wills and inheritance? I'm used to it; after all I married into it.

Grandpa once said to me, "You mean to tell me that your first wife was Jewish, too!!?"

"Yes."

"What the hell is the matter with you!?"

I said, "Hey, I decided a long time ago, that I did not want to make any decisions on my own."

*** But still you try. ***

"Shut up, Jack."

*** You can still make them when she's not here, but then you'd still be wrong. ***

155

They made Jay and I play as scratch. Jay came in 2 under so they had to squeeze out three bucks to each one in our foursome. Grandpa laughed as the treasurer struggled.

"What's so funny?"

"Did you actually think you were going to take their money, today?' Grandpa laughed. "They can drive the par fours on a fly."

"Yeah well next time they play as plus 5.", as old Ben strangled the third dollar onto the pile.

I picked up one of the dollar bills and it said, "Happy Bar Mitzvah, Benny" on it.

"I'd frame that one if I were you." Grandpa said as Jay and I laughed all the way home.

"Hey, Jack, I won three bucks."

*** Really? You spent 2 dollars in tolls and 4 bucks in gas to get here and back. Do the math! ***

"Yeah but Jay drove."

*** You really are a cheap bastard. ***

It Puts the Rules on its Skin

The only relief you get from poison ivy comes in a jar. The USGA rules are like the tax-code and if you are unscrupulous enough you can either use them to your advantage or make up a few as you go. I did not always know all the rules but as I got more familiar with them I realized that I had been duped a few times. I'm sure I am not alone. My friend Harry says, "We play the ball down because otherwise people will take liberties." In light of some experiences it is hard to disagree.

I took our annual golf trip to Ocean City, Maryland. It's a land of beautiful sandy beaches and across the bridge there are lakes and streams surrounded by snakes, ticks, thorns, bees and poisonous plants. This is where they put all of their golf courses.

One of our members was becoming a teaching pro. It is easier than you think; it has to be because this guy sucks. He had passed all the rules tests so he considered himself an authority. We always considered him to be a pain in the ass. When he said, "I get relief from this nest of bees." No one would question him. And when he said, "This is poison ivy." He took relief and we let him do it because we are subservient rules-morons, you know, beta golfers living under the shadow of his royal hind-ass; the alleged pro.

There is no shortage of people who will try to bend the rules or invent rules in their favor. Just as in politics you have the self-appointed Speaker-of-the-house who professes to know the rules and if one does not exist, once again they will invent one.

Recently I had a person tell me, "You can't tap a putt in with the back of your putter." It is hard to watch a pro event without someone doing exactly that. It is legal.

"You have to use the same club that you are going to use to measure your drop." Nay-nay!

"If you take relief because your only shot is left handed you have to hit the ball left-handed after you take relief…" Wrong, wrong, wrong.

This one I got when I called the assistant pro for a ruling, "Your ball must be more than half-way in its own pitch-mark to get relief." Wrong again.

If you are not sure of the rule, these are your best options:

1. Your ball – play it as it lies
2. Competitor's ball –shut your beer hole until you look up the rule.

On my second day with my men's club in Florida one of the guys hit a palm tree; the ball came down with a vengeance and plugged in a closely mown area. I am a fan of the guys that I play with and am in favor of justifiable relief. Although I stated the rule, the more senior member said "There is no relief. We play the ball down here."

It is painful. But what is more painful is that on the very next hole this same strict constructionist back handed a putt, hit the ground instead of the ball and never charged himself with a stroke. Counting on your opponent to inform you when he breaks a rule is like leaving Vegas with more money than you came with. I should have called him on it but my newness to the club kept me quiet.

*** That and the fact that he was bigger than you. ***

There is a rule that says that you cannot give wrong information, like the wrong score for example. There is also a rule that says that you are not allowed to suggest or offer advice. An incorrect ruling by a fellow-competitor could be construed as a poor recommendation, but lacking any actual USGA rule, it must be considered as "advice"; poor as it might be. There is, in fact, a USGA rule 8-1 that provides for a two-stroke penalty for giving advice. It would and should be levied upon any asshole that wrongfully punishes a fellow-competitor with a wrongful and or a non-existent ruling. So I am making a ruling, an interpretation if you will, that says, "If you misquote a rule that adversely affects your competitor, you must incur a 2-stroke penalty or loss of hole in match play. It seems fair, right Jack?

*** Quid pro quo, Clarice; quid pro quo.[4] ***

Walking Crows

We've got this guy at the club and I am sure you have a few like him. He loves…no, he lives to argue.

"How much do you weigh?" He'll ask.

---

[4] Jack is bastardizing a conversation between psycho Hannibal Lecter and FBI agent Clarice Starling in the movie "Silence of the Lambs".

I am neither skinny nor fat so I really don't care what I weigh. "One-seventy." I answer matter-of-factly.

"No, you don't!"

"Fine, I weigh something else then; now get lost."

An opportunity for any discussion is lost as he walks away in disgust. A shrink would carefully point out that he cannot win an argument at home. I get this image of him looking up obscure facts to argue about. The members are victims and the course is his hood. But at least, I'll give him this; he takes the time to get his facts.

Political opinions vary but the American Indians label them best as "Walking Crows".

** Because they are too full of shit to fly! **

6: Get a Life

I retired at 55 and I found myself playing golf almost every day and if I wasn't playing I practiced. I practiced before I went out and after I came in. I have OCD, ADD, ADHD and I am workaholic with all of the TLAs (Three Letter Acronyms) you wish to add. Workaholic may be a bit over the top; a hedonistic play-aholic is probably closer. I was putting in at least 60 hours a week on the course. My hands dried out, cracked and bled from the crap they spread on the greens to kill whatever moves. I slept with Vaseline soaked hands in cotton gloves, got up, showered, had breakfast and hit the links. I taped my fingers wherever the latest cut showed up and then chipped and putted for hours waiting for a game.

My company was still paying my salary for a year; even my club membership. I was not sure that they knew that last part. They are a big company with 30,000 employees in over 200 countries. My membership was doing the under-the-radar limbo until some idiot rocked the boat. The course owners found a financial wizard and put him in charge.   They raised the monthly dues so naturally that went before my company's board of directors for approval. And that was the end of my stealth membership

I had been with the company over 20 years and it was a nice reward which I accepted gratefully. I knew it would not last so I milked it for all that I could. I even opened my wallet for lessons. I got down to a low handicap and set a target to get down to Jay's level. My cell phone rang but it wasn't Jay.

** *Get real!* **

Jack was right; I had forgotten that as great as it is, this is really only a game. You have to be careful with your audience with your lofty goals. It is something you keep to yourself or use as advice when someone throws a putter in the drink. It should be someone smaller than you and someone who is not familiar with any of the martial arts.

I have had delusions of great possible accomplishments in a warning-track-power body for my whole life. After superb coaching from Jack I achieved enlightenment; I stopped playing and practicing. I did some projects around the house to ensure that my hands still knew how to dry up and bleed. I had some insidious weeds so I got some stuff from our greenskeeper to spread on my lawn. It really did take care of the weeds and the skin on my hands. Maybe it was because I missed the Vaseline and the cotton gloves.

** *Pervert!* **

I cut back on my golf and my expectations. I only played on Saturday mornings with my regular group. My handicap started to climb. No, no, no, no, this was a good thing! As a low handicap, I was losing money every week. I did not win a game. When I moved up a few notches my handicap rose and I started to win now and then. I looked forward to a few beers at the end of a round. It was then that I got a text message from an anonymous party.

** Welcome back to the fold. **

"Thanks Jack."

** Sandbagger! **

"I did not know that you knew that term."

** Oh I keep up with all of the insult slang. **

Guilty Partners

I may have to go back a bit in time to put this in perspective. Golf was an intermission. An instance when was something was needed to deter the boredom and occupy my time. This was before I felt a need for a "regular game".

I would peel my clubs off the garage wall and go to the town's obligatory Brentwood Country Club. If my wife did not feel like being dumped out of the cart or drop a club on my head I would go alone. I had just started playing more regularly and I was quick enough to be decent company. I would pay the green fees and wheel my cart to the starter's booth. At a public course the starter is Caesar, and if you want to play that same day you better pay him tribute. It is written that if you are Irish and your hair turns gray you must take a job as a starter; George fit that part nicely.

165

"I poot ya wit deese tree lads. Aye, day be faidr playez each one."

I translated that and said "Thanks, George." as I gave him a buck.

"Dare now. Tanks for dat."

As I walked over to greet them I heard, a distant noise that sounded like "Cheap Bastit".

Hmmm, was that George or Jack imitating George?

Chuck, Hugh and Farley knew each other from one place or another and they all had golf in common. They were all decent golfers so it made for a pretty good round. From a distance it probably looked like a dad having a round of golf with his three kids. Hugh, Chuck and I are about the same size give or take an inch. Farley is noticeably bigger. His hair is prematurely gray and look a bit like Leslie Nielson but much taller. His reddish complexion reveals someone who plays a lot or maybe drinks or both. His swing was true to the evidence as he smacked a beauty down the middle with a little tight draw like he hadn't a care in the world.

Hugh's hair is dark and a bit long. He is too thin and his feet bail out as if he were thrown a vicious curve when he swings. Even so he manages good club head speed. He hit a fade down the left side that landed down the middle near Farley's ball.

Chuck has black hair and a good sized belly; maybe Lou Costello sets the right picture but a shade thinner. Chuck has a compact swing and hit the straightest ball I'd ever seen. His tee shot was a good one right down the middle.

I followed with a little draw slightly larger than Farley's. Oddly enough the four balls were so close you could have fit them in a pizza box. This was odd, not because of the distance, but because some of us would not see the fairway again until the back nine.

One could say we played in order of height. Farley shot a 77. The rest of us struggled to break 90. We had a nice round and stopped at the bar. Our laughter was directly in line with the number of beers as we made plans for next weekend.

I joined them at Swan Lake that following week and we were becoming fast friends. Chuck would hit a nice chip followed by Farley's "Nice up Chuck."

Golf brings out the best of all of us when we first meet people. You're on your best behavior; you're courteous and as helpful as an ass-kisser at the office. But once you get to know the guys you play with, the gloves come off. There is that certain level of meanness that lurks within all of us. You can mix this in with those funny but hurtful things you think of at the wrong time. Most people have the restraint to keep these comments to themselves. I do not have that luxury nor do I hold to that kind of discipline. I just blurt stuff out.

I am not sure where this comes from, probably years of Catholic school restraint bubbling out like intestinal gas. I flat-out cannot help myself; kind of an oral

167

flatulence. Chuck hit a fat shot that went about twenty yards falling short of the water and I added, "Really? I would never have thought of laying up from there."

Or I'd scull a wedge and Hugh would offer, "I really liked that shot until you hit it."

Or Hugh would ask, "Did I go in the water?"

"Not yet." Chuck struck back.

It is not meant to cut deeply. It's not sarcasm. It is just meant to amuse someone, even if it is only for my own amusement.

"Do you think I can get there with a five iron?"

"Eventually."

Sometimes people leave themselves open and when this happens, you have an obligation to just fire away. I know I do.

"What is wrong with my game?"

"Probably the 20 inches between your ears."

I've had golf lessons and if I could afford them I'd get more. As I said my dad used to brag that he never took one lesson and the English guy said, "That explains it then." So this blurting out of the cutting remarks is not something that I own. Golf lends itself to our best and our very poorest behavior; it is addictive.

Once, looking out over the water at a 150 yard par three, my wife asked me, "What do you think I should use on this hole."

"How about a sleeve of balls. ….Oh, uh, sorry, honey, I meant do you need a sleeve of balls, sweetie. I've got plenty here in my bag. Use your five-iron, dear."

*** You're just a freakin' sissy at heart, admit it. ***

Golf Vacations

Each week the four of us got better and better, but we were still not as consistent as Farley. We stopped for the obligatory beer ritual of recounting our shots. I don't mean re-adding them, I mean describing the difficulty and the success of them.

"Like I say to my wife, forget the bad ones." I'd add.

"Just remember to count them" Hugh laughed as he remembered the story I told him.

"Maybe Wayne would like to join us in Myrtle Beach in April." Farley added.

"Sounds good, I'll check with Stephanie."

Jack would have some kind of comment on my reply but my comment went unchallenged. Maybe he found other prey. I said my goodbyes and walked out to my car. As I opened the door a few leaves rustled.

*** Pussy? *** Jack said and then continued one octave higher. *** Oh, I'll check with Stephanie. ***

"Hi Jack!"

*** Hi Jack? Too bad we're not at the airport with that come back! Love to see you in cuffs. ***

"Bet you would, you pervert! "

*** Ah, that's more like it. ***

"Where have you been?"

*** You're not the only person on this planet. I have other people to annoy. My mother-in-law was in town. ***

Who Knows Jack

I'm not sure how it occurred or in what order. We did agree to go Myrtle Beach and definitive plans were made for four of us. Hugh was going to drive his father-in-law's van down with his wife, Jamie, so I brought Stephanie.

*** Pussy. *** Jack reminded me followed by the crack of a whip.

"Don't you have some small child to annoy?"

*** They're much too quick for me. You're more fun. ***

The girls met for the first time in this long ride to South Carolina from Long Island. Jamie is tall and even looks a bit like Jamie Lee Curtis except she has long hair. Her height is in contrast to my 5'2" curly blonde haired wife. They hit it off immediately and became the best of friends. This allowed Hugh and me to take many golf trips together without the guilt or having Jack calling us names. We all packed the van to the hilt, unloaded it and repacked it. When we were satisfied that there was no way Hugh would be able to see out the back we closed the hatch.

"There! That oughta do it." Jamie said.

Stephanie and I sat in the back because there is an order of things in this world. When people first meet the couples sit with each other. The next time they meet, the husbands sit in the front and the women sit in the back. When the husbands get snot-slinging drunk the seating is reversed. I don't make these rules; that's just how it's done.

I had quit cigarettes before I met Hugh so naturally the three of them smoked the entire 14 hours of the trip. It's like yawning, if one person lit a cigarette the other two joined in. The conversation went something like this:

"You guys are killing me!"

"Oh, here we go; another militant ex-smoker."

"Roll down your window."

"Fine."

Nothing quite compares with that awful noise an open back window delivers at 70 mile per hour. You can simulate this by cupping both your hands and slapping your ears repeatedly. I tried this to make sure I gave that the right description. My wife looked at me like I completely lost my mind. So you might want to try this in private or just take my word for it. I decided I would rather choke to death than have my ears boxed for the rest of the trip.

"Cigarettes are really cheap in the Carolina's."

"Oh great, just great!" I managed to choke out.

** I don't smell anything. **

"So why are you complaining then?" Jamie asked.

"Holy shit", I thought, "Did Jamie hear Jack!?"

** Uh, oh! No, no, no wait a minute this could be really good. **

I'm thinking, while it's nice to have confirmation of Jack's existence, Jack sees this as a golden opportunity to pull my chain. No, no, no, this cannot be good at all.

** I'll have to practice my best Wayne imitation. **

Breakfast at Two Funnies

The girls were not playing golf; they would do 'their thing' whatever that means. Farley drove his brand new Jeep Grand Cherokee down with Derek. Chuck could not make it so Farley found another perfectly good weirdo to fill our foursome. Derek was our normal average sized replacement with dark hair, glasses and a trace of a mustache but he was thin. If he wanted to replace Chuck he needed to add about 50 pounds. Derek drank coffee all day. If I had 12 beers Derek would match me with coffee. The next morning most of us headed down for breakfast at a table for six but we were only five.

"He was so wired he took his mattress and put it up against the wall." Farley had said and then added, "He hit golf balls into it all night long and, at some point, he fell asleep on the floor. Luckily I am not a light sleeper."

"Is he coming down for breakfast?" Stephanie asked.

"No he said he wants to sleep until we leave for golf but to bring him back a …."

"…another cup of coffee." Jamie finished as we all laughed.

When I was a kid 'a good hearty breakfast' meant a few eggs, bacon, maybe some home-fries and buttered toast. The proverbial 'they' go back and forth on whether it's healthy or not. The waitress came over and the rapid fire conversation started.

"Good morning…..what'll it be..?" The waitress was already tired of the repetition. Her badge said her name was Theresa. That's a good warning not to call her Terry.

"I'm not ready." Stephanie said.

"I'll have two eggs over, bacon extra crispy and burn the potatoes." Jamie said.

"I'll have the same." Steph said.

"Make that three."

"Make it four."

"I'll have the Eggs Benedict but I'd like the potatoes burnt too."

"It doesn't come with potatoes." She said.

"Make it five of the same then."

"Five coffees?" Theresa asked as four heads nodded.

"Tea for me." Stephanie said.

"Four coffees and a tea." Waiting for no further comments, she spun around and headed for the kitchen.

I swear that entire conversation took no more than 30 seconds. The breakfast however did not show up for almost 30 minutes. The eggs were over hard, the bacon was burnt to a crisp and the potatoes were mildly browned.

"I'd like to send this back if she promises not to spit on it" I said.

"She could promise anything, just eat it." Steph replied.

Stephanie and I both worked in separate restaurants, in different states at different times together but we both agreed on one thing: Never, ever piss off the people who serve your food. If you must send something back, tell them that *you* made a mistake and ordered it wrong. We all decided that since this breakfast came free with the hotel it would not get better with age. The next day we would pay to eat somewhere else. We left a shitty tip for two reasons, the service sucked and it was my turn to leave it.

The next morning we ordered the same thing except for one eggs benedict with a side of allowable home fries. This was perfect. Even Derek joined us.

"Theresa sucks the big one." Jamie said.

"Cheers." As we all toasted our coffees and one tea.

"Who's Theresa?" Derek managed between sips.

"Never mind." Farley said. "You'll never see her again, I mean, at all …ever."

"Oh? Ohhh!" Derek seemed concerned that Farley, his boss, had done something illegal to this 'Theresa'.

The look on Derek's face was priceless and Farley shrugged, smiled, sipped his coffee and scratched his chin like Don Corleone[5]. Hugh and I were laughing so hard I think I pulled a cheek muscle. The girls just looked at us, then at each other, shrugged and sipped their drinks. They were off to the zoo and we were ready for another day of golf.

Enough Already

In between these two breakfasts we managed to play some golf, eat lunch, dinner and drank 'til we dropped. Stephanie usually doesn't drink but Jamie is a terrific influence and they had a blast.

As far as the golf went, there was irony. We had all driven from Long Island where the winter's chill was still lingering this first week of April. We drove 600 miles south to find the same damned weather in Myrtle Beach!! This day was also garnished with a nice cold drizzle to complete the discomfort. No matter, we drove all this way and we are playing golf, damn it! I had bought a really nice, expensive rain suit. Gortex was just invented.

---

[5] Don Corleone – forget it - if I have to explain this it's not going to be funny.

It was probably more money than I should have spent but Stephanie would not have it any other way.

So here we are at Waterway Hills on a rain soaked first tee box. Farley is up first and takes a few practice swings, not down the fairway, but in our direction. I am not sure why people do that. Maybe they are claiming the land, "This tee box is mine" or maybe they just need some space. Farley's third practice swing was a bit fat; chunky, if you know what I mean. A hunk of mud-filled sod hits my chest, splatters my pants and a good part of my face.

** Wait! What good part of your face? **

Okay, fine!! But it hit my face and I looked at Farley with both palms up as if to ask, "What the hell?" as the sod chunk falls from my face to my open palm, the one with the brand new glove on it.

To remove any misunderstanding, I said out loud, "What the f**k?"

"Oh, sorry'. A pathetic plea came from Farley's direction but it might have been Derek.

You could tell that Farley felt really bad. He hit his tee shot right down the middle as a disguise but he could not hide the guilt. I could tell. I got an old glove out of my bag and wiped myself off with Farley's brand new towel and put it on his seat muddy side down. I felt bad about that too and hit my drive past Farley's as I tried to hide my bubbling red-ass remorse.

Derek was a bit nervous playing with his boss. He took out some kind of wood other than a driver and hit it short but down the middle.

"Why didn't you hit your driver?" I asked

"I can't hit the damned thing."

"So why do you carry one?" Hugh asked.

"It came with the set."

Hugh stepped up, took a few practice swings at Farley for my entertainment but did not raise even a blade of grass. He turned toward the ball and smacked a beauty. He was on target with his tee shot so now most of us were in good shape for the moment. Farley retrieved his towel and wiped the seat with the muddy side and gave me a look.

"Gee, I wonder where this came from?" He gestured as he displayed the towel.

"If I were a betting man I'd say from your driver; maybe not directly."

It was "cart path only" and that was at least one rule we would obey. We took off down the path and tried to guess which clubs to walk across to our respective balls.

*** Respective Balls? ***

"Shut up Jack, Where were you when Farley gave me the mud bath."

*** I was laughing too hard to talk. ***

It seemed that Hugh and I played against Farley alone. Farley's partner, Derek, was of no help in our little "best ball" match.

"Don't even go there Jack!"

Derek was playing the best he could but Farley was always at least one stroke better. Hugh and I made pars, bogeys and double bogeys on different holes keeping us tied with Farley. We played like brothers-in-law and then a real miracle occurred. I hit a decent drive with only a nine-iron to the ninth green. I sunk it for my first eagle ever. Well not counting Brentwood 17. That's the shortest par 5 and probably not sanctioned by the USGA. So not counting that, this was my first real eagle. This meant that Hugh and I had won the front nine. Those two dollars were ours to share. It's not the money; it is about the bragging rights.

*** It's the money you cheap bastard. ***

"Hey Jack, how about that eagle?"

*** Enjoy this brief moment. ***

I shot a 39 on the front and a handsome 49 on the back as my game fell apart to Jack's total amusement. Hugh picked me up on every hole but Derek woke up. There was no coffee at the turn so he had a few beers instead. If Farley made a mistake on the back Derek was there with a par or birdie. Derek shot a 38 on the back. I had one shining moment; I had a par on 17 and Derek made birdie. Hugh played well and shot a 40 but we lost the back by two, the overall by one, the bragging rights and two bucks a piece.

*** It IS about the money you cheap bastard. ***

"How about that eagle?"

*** That moment is gone. ***

When I got back to the hotel they gave me a trophy for my eagle. I'd never seen any hotel do that but it was very nice.

"Well, isn't this nice, Jack?"

*** Oh good grief! ***

Crab Zipper

That night we split from Farley and Derek to take the girls out alone. Steph found a place that had all the King Crab you can eat. Back then $29.95 was a lot for any buffet but we figured, hey King Crab, how could we go wrong?

The one thing about King Crag is that it has a nasty shell and this restaurant picked the hardest, spiniest king crabs allowed by law. Since it was all you can eat you had to crack them yourself. They had no nutcrackers. What a surprise. It was like trying to pull a tooth out of a porcupine with your bare hands. And as your hands got soaking wet they got softer and almost impossible to snap a crab leg without screaming. What no one knew was that Hugh once worked at a King Crab canning

179

factory in Alaska. He could take a regular table fork, find the right seam and open each leg like they had a zipper. Hugh opened one after another faster than the four of us could eat them. After our third round the manager came over.

"Can I get anyone more corn on the cob, maybe some bread, more beer or maybe would you like your desert now? He seemed to be begging.

"No, no thanks."

"We're good. Thanks."

"Maybe another plate of those crab legs?" Jamie fired over his bow.

"Yeah, I could eat one more." Steph joined in.

I was too busy eating and Hugh had zipped eight more legs open during this brief conversation. Doing his eat one zip four; eat one zip four-routine to the horror of the manager.   He walked off shaking his head as he whispered something to the waitress.

She brought us a stingy plate of legs, corn on the cob, potatoes, bread and a nice salad that went to waste. I was so stuffed. I had half a beer left and when I went to take a sip I found that there was no place for it to go. I put it back down and even Jack cried for me.

*** Uncle. ***

"Oh are you giving up?" Jamie said.

"Uh, yeah." I said. Thinking, that proves it; she can definitely hear Jack.

"Me, too.' Hugh and Steph agreed.

Hugh held up this bent fork. "I wonder how much they are going to charge us for this bent fork."

"Nothing." I said as I grabbed it, bent it back close to its original shape and switched it with a clean fork from the table next to ours. The waitress came over a few moments later.

"Would you like your desert, maybe some coffee?"

"No, no thanks, we couldn't swallow another bite. Just the check, please."

She came back with the check within seconds, "I'll take that whenever you are ready."

We paid her and left a good tip. As we got to the door Stephanie said, "She forgot to say, come back again real soon."

*** Go figure? ***

"Yeah, go figure." Jamie laughed.

I whispered aside, "A momentous occasion, Jack; someone got the last word on you."

*** Bite me. ***

Hugh and I were too full to talk. I was afraid if I opened my mouth something might jump out. We waddled back to the hotel and walked right by an ice cream place. It took twice the normal time to get there. Now I know why manatees move the way they do.

When we got back to the hotel, I finally spoke, "I think I may skip breakfast tomorrow."

"Why, are you planning on hitting some balls into the mattress tonight?" Jamie kidded.

"Gee that's pretty personal don't you think?" as I teased her back. "I think that I will not have fully digested dinner until sometime around noon tomorrow.

*** Maybe just a coffee then, Derek? ***

Jamie and I laughed at Jack's little joke. Then she realized that I did not say that and looked both ways and behind us and then at me. I shrugged and then she started to laugh again.

"It wasn't that funny." Hugh said and added. "I hope I can swing a club tomorrow."

"Manish Tanah ha-laylah ha-ze mi kol ha-leylot?" Stephanie asked.

"What does that mean?" Hugh asked.

"It's Hebrew, it actually means "Why is tonight any different from any other night?" Or tomorrow for that matter." Steph explained.

We all laughed but in the morning the jokes were on us. We were all slow to rise but we did manage to get to breakfast. Since we were only having coffee we went to the free breakfast bar, got our own beverages and sat at table. About 15 minutes later the speedy Theresa came to our table to take our order just as we were walking out.

*** We'll have six eggs benedicts. ***

Yes and burn the potatoes." Jamie said.

"Huh?' Theresa was perplexed.

** Thanks, Jamie. **

Jamie replied, "You're welcome. Wayne, you heard that too right?"

"Heard what?"

"Hmmm?" Jamie wrinkled her nose as if she was bewitched.

But I wasn't ready to give Jack away or any credit at least not yet; people might have me put away. So the girls went off to do their thing and we met up with Farley and his faithful employee. I had forgotten that we had to play 36 holes. I needed four emergency stops at the men's room and twice as many stops to buy beer from the cart girl.

Cart Girls – the Good, the Bad and Doral

Did you ever take a walk down Main Street and see a place like a basket shop or maybe a ribbon store. I catch myself thinking, "How the hell can they pay the rent?" A few months later that store would have a brand new sign, "Space for Rent".

That's kind of the way I think about a beverage cart on a golf course. I understand the profit for the golf course but what about the driver. I mean somewhere in a remote planet some youth might say, "When I grow up I am going to be a cart girl."

If you own a ribbon shop downtown you could run numbers or make book in the back room but a golf cart has no such area. These beer-tenders are an independent lot and they come in all shapes, sizes and demeanors. There are good ones, great ones and then there are those that make you blurt out, "who hired that bitch!!?" Once in a while you will see a beverage cart guy. Yeah, there's a real money-maker!

Any experienced cart-cutie knows to travel the course backwards. You can tell a novice as she comes up behind you on your backswing. "You guys need anything!!?"

The carts are usually beat into submission by a person who does not know the open end of a wrench or care. But sometimes you run into that unique individual that is a gold mine to any country club. A savvy food and beverage manager knows that a pretty girl that is happy at her job will sell twice the beer than their bartender and if math is within her skills, you have a lucky charm.

Some are busy texting their boyfriends and you may see them once on each nine holes; the good ones you will see at least twice on each side. The fastest and best I've ever seen was at Colony West in Tamarac, Florida. You will see her six or seven times a round. That's a lot of beer. She is quick but some of the credit or debit has to go with the typical six-hour round of the traffic jam known as Colony West. The course, the cart-girl, the drinks and the food are exceptional but the pace of play needs work. One thing we have learned across the board is that heavy tipping has little effect on a slow cart girl.

*** What a surprise! ***

"Oh come on Jack, Hugh over tips the good looking ones but that doesn't make the girl skip the other guys. Slow is slow."

*** True, but you're still a cheap bastard. ***

At the course you will see the guy at the counter and the starter only once, but if the place has shitty management the cart girl will be the first to let you know.

"How's it going today?"

"Two more hours and I am #%# outta here."

You can also tell how many times you will see her based on this first conversation. You know whether her boss is a real asshole or not. And then of course there are the prices.

I was at Doral in Miami. My friend Mike got a free foursome from his friend Art. Usually one has to go to Jamaica to be robbed on the golf course. But here in Miami, the Blue Monster will reach into your wallet and pull out $350 a person. The only difference is that you are not looking down the barrel of a loaded gun. But not today; today we play for free.

Ah, but not so fast my fortunate son! Just in case you think you are going to get away cheap they send out the cart girl.

"Good morning gentlemen. What will you have today?" she says as she flips her suspiciously blonde hair and a sales pitch that any gold-digger would be proud of.

"Hey, Mike, you got us this freebee, let me buy the drinks." I said.

** *What?* ** was followed by a thud.

I think Jack fainted.

"Okay, I'll have a Bloody Mary." Mike said.

"Make it two.' said Jon.

"Make it three." Jeff said.

"Okay, four Bloody Mary's, please."

She took out four 16 ounce Styrofoam cups, filled them with ice, unscrewed four airplane Smirnoff's and topped them off with some premixed tomato product.

"Will that be all?"

"Yes, thanks." As I squeezed out a hundred.

"Here's your change." She said as she matter-of-factly handed me a ten and two fives.

"I gave you a hundred."

"I know; they are 20 dollars apiece."

Now Jack was steadying me. "You are kidding, right?"

"Nope, sorry."

She had this expression that told me that most of the people here would have said, "Keep the change."

I gave her a ten. Even Jack was silent.

"Thanks." She said as she left.

I prayed that I would not see her more than two more times. Jeff and Jon could take their turn before I'd have to peel off another Franklin.

The perfect ounce and a half of vodka was hidden by ice and other liquids.

"I should have asked for a double!" Mike said.

*** Cha ching. ***

I did not exactly explain the episode to the other guys. I was not sure it was my place. But when Mike thought about a double, I had to say something.

"Uh, they charged 20 apiece for a single. I think she has to account for the liquor so it might me 40 apiece for a double."

"No, really?"

"Welcome to Doral." Jon said.

She came back way too quickly. I figured a lot of people waved her off on the way. Jon got the next round but we changed our drinks to something less concocted. I had a beer. I did not ask what it cost.

If you are a client on someone else's company dime have them take you to South Beach. The sights are outrageous; the prices are as heavy as the clothing is skimpy and you can buy one Corona for the price of a twelve pack.

The Blue Monster at Doral is not the most challenging course in South Florida; it is not in the best of shape, the food is not five-star and everything, including water and range balls are a la carte. But you get to say you played Doral or should I say, Doral played you.

7: While We're Still Young

You remember my Coors-light friend John. This is a man that speeds up play naturally. John is a man's man. He sits in the cart and drinks but when it's his turn he is ready. He takes no practice swing and hits the ball as soon as his feet are set. He fixes his divot and gets back in the cart with this towel and his club; then we take off for the next shot. After we finish the hole he gets back in the cart with his putter. John is ready for action; he does not sashay his way through life to smell the roses. John is a man of action. John was in charge of all sales for a major car company for the entire East Coast of the U.S.

"I'll wait and put this club back when I am ready to take out the next one I need."

His efficiency is inescapable. His logic cannot be questioned by more sober men of which they are plenty but they remain slugs just the same.

*** This is a game slowed down by too much thought. ***

Eighty-Six These Guys

The number 86 in the restaurant business means, "We are all out." We are all out of scallops, shrimp or whatever. The kitchen uses this to tell the help not to take any more orders for that dish. I am going to use this number to mean "We are 86 on slow play!"

The PGA and the LPGA have taken this up in commercials. They have taken a quote by Rodney

Dangerfield, "While we're still young!" from the movie Caddy Shack.

This is the stuff that slows the game down and aggravates playing partners and especially the foursome behind you. So while I am still young Jack will help me with a few 86 stories.

The CPA

In golf, a CPA is really a "constant pain in the ass". This guy writes the scores down when he gets off the green. He sits in the cart, looks back down the fairway and points to recount each of his shots. He asks everyone else what they had so he can write it down because he might forget before he gets to the next tee box. This guy needs to go to a memory clinic before I bounce one off his roof.

** Hey taxman! Get your ass over to the next tee before April 15th and figure this out! **

The Hammer Throw

You don't have to play this game too long to see someone down the fairway or on the green losing control. It is a very frustrating game. It is almost comical unless you are in close proximity. I've flipped, tossed and launched a whirly-bird or two in my time. Jack was quick enough to point out the character flaw in that.

*** Asshole comes to mind. ***

I saw Dad's boss break, throw and mutilate a set of clubs during a round. I did not make me think that he was rich and could afford it. Any thought that he was a good golfer was completely erased by his loud tirades. He almost hit me with a nine iron. So then next time Dad asked me if I wanted to join them I just said, "No, thanks."

And Dad replied, "Lucky you."

No one has ever looked impressive by throwing a club.

*** Oh I don't know about that! I get a lot of enjoyment watching Tiger throw a club and quite often. ***

Men of the Opposite Sex

I've played with guys with head covers on their irons. I've played golf with guys who wipe their clubs after every shot. I even know guys who wash their clubs after every round. Individually these seem quite normal but collectively performed on the course is beyond meticulous. Let's just call this guy Felix.

Felix brushes, wet wipes, dry towels and covers his club after every shot? This would even still be tolerable if he wiped his club after a practice swing. This only slows us down a bit. Felix places his zebra-striped head cover on top of the bag and it blends in with the other striped covers in his bag. After his annoying club wash-rinse-dry-and-fold routine he pauses and looks to me for support.

"Did you see my cover?"

I lean my head on the steering wheel as I shake my head back and forth.

"We'll have to drive back; I can't find my head cover. I've got to have my head cover."

Now we drive back and of course we do not find it. We ask the group behind us who already have their shotguns out.

I tell him, "Someone will turn it in, I'm sure."

We head back to the green. Felix is now twitching at the thought of a lost head cover. As he goes back to grab his putter Felix says, "Oh here's my head cover! It was on the top of my other clubs all along."

I Lizzy-Borden'ed him with my putter and I was only charged with 40 strokes and time served.

*** He'll be dead now about a year next Tuesday. ***

The Turtle and the Snail

I played with this guy for a few weeks and he always got to the course before me. Naturally he got the cart and the driver's seat that went with it. He always parks the cart on the side of the green away from the next tee.

If there is anything efficient that can be done with a golf cart he will avoid it.

The other two guys we are with are walking and they were beating us. I don't mean the score; I mean the speed. If this cart moved any slower we would only exist in an alternate dimension. I looked over at Tom and his foot barely depressed the accelerator.

"Foot cramp?" I asked.

"No, why do you ask?"

"This cart is going slower than Gary and he's walking."

"You know more accidents on the golf course are caused by golf carts than golf balls by far."

"Does that include sudden fits of frustration and backseat driver beatings?"

Tommy the Turtle ignores my comments and swings over to my ball which is 35 yards ahead of his. Somewhere in the depths of his natural inefficiency he excuses this behavior as a matter of "courtesy".

No matter; I am ready to hit my ball. I turn to Tom and say, "Why don't you go to your ball? I'll hit mine and then you will be ready to hit yours."

As a final admission Tom reveals the source of all of his unholy existence, "Oh that's okay. I'm not in any hurry."

I hit my ball, replace my divot and return in the cart with my club. When we finally get to Tom's ball he paced off the distance to the 150 marker.

"I've got a range finder Tom." I said. "You're 145 out."

"I've got one too but you can't trust those things; besides this is faster and more accurate."

"Really, Tom…faster…more accurate?"

*** Tom got attacked by snails by the pond. When they asked him what happened he said, "I don't know; it all happened so fast. ***

Slow Moe

You get paired up with this guy but something seems a bit "off" right from the very start. You're next on the tee. He arrives late and he says he has to go "potty". Most people put their best foot forward when they first meet but like I said, you cannot hide; golf finds the real you. Moe's way of doing things seemed odd from the start but I could not place it.

*** He's living in slow-motion. ***

"That's it! Good catch, Jack."

*** Think nothing of it. Actually it would be best if you didn't think. ***

When you're out on the course he spends an inordinate amount of time slowly preparing for his shot. The video-tape replay which is Moe's life is only interrupted by intermittent freeze-frames as he comes to a complete halted stance over the ball. Nothing is happening; not a thing!?

Maybe this is his super-slow-mo'; maybe I should switch to time-lapse but wait... suddenly I see the club come back, then down as he stubs the ball about five and a half feet. He looks at me as if I had contributed to his misfortune. He wipes the mud from each groove on his club before he starts the painful slug walk and routine once more.

** I'll get a rope; you find a tree. **

You've played five holes with him and the group in front of you is already a hole ahead. It's your first time with *his royal sloth-ness* so you try to be as polite as you can. Moe inch worms his way back to his bag after another bad shot.

"I am off my game today." He says excusing his bad play.

** He knows he can play better than this, he just never has. **

"Maybe it's you're timing?"

"Could be; you think I should slow down?"

"No, no, no...I did not mean that at all. Look! The group in front of us has finished the next hole. Maybe we can try to keep up, you know, move a little faster. Maybe you should hit the ball when you get into your stance before all of those negative waves get inside your head. Try it."

"Okay, I don't like to be rushed but I'll try."

"Good. That's great, thanks."

It worked. He actually made a good shot. After three good shots in a row, I thought we made a new golfer out of Moe. But then it happened; Moe dubbed a bad shot like the ones he had been hitting all day. He took two steps toward his bag and slid back one. He added the club back in his bag along with the final straw.

"You see? This is what happens when I am rushed! I play lousy when I'm rushed; the hell with your stupid timing!"

"So you believe that you play better when you are slow and throw off everyone else's timing?"

"Yeah well I am not going to be rushed! You play your game your way and I will play my way."

"I cannot play my way! I play fast and you play too slow. I feel like we teed off yesterday."

"I'd like to set up a race between you and Tommy the Turtle?"

Moe grabs a hold of his towel and throws it down. "I refuse to be rushed!"

** Oh one day you will be rushed, one day for sure. I already have the rope. **

The Never Ready Battery

To be ready means being prepared, equipped, organized and all set. David Leadbottom was none of those things. His lack of thought process is evident. Leadbottom will sit in the cart, wait for everyone else to hit and then and only then will he put down his coffee and slide his fat ass out of the cart and then he goes through his exhausting routine.

He pulls out his range finder and zaps the flag.

"135, hmmm, what does yours say?"

"Mine says hit the damn ball already."

David L. takes out his iron, walks over and addresses his ball. He takes not one but three practice swings. He wipes the face of the club and stands over the ball. He stands over the ball and nothing is happening.

So much time has passed and yet he remains motionless over the ball. I am thinking that a Hail Mary takes about 13 seconds; an Our Father takes about 20 and a Novena takes 8 days. Somewhere in between he must be reciting something. Forty-five seconds had gone by when suddenly a pigeon flew over and landed on his shoulder. It took a nice white shit on him and then flew away. Ironically it did not mess up Leadbottom, his routine or his concentration. My laughter at the sight however bothered him immensely.

"Do you MIND!? Please keep quiet while I go through my routine."

"Cloistered monks are not expected to be quiet that long!!"

So he started all over. When he reached for his range finder Jack picked it up and boomed.

*** DON'T EVEN THINK ABOUT IT! ***

I don't know if it was the floating range finder or if David L. actually heard Jack. He went immediately over to his ball and shanked it about 30 yards.

His voice mocked his shaking hands as he got back into the cart with his club.

"Did you…did you see…see what I saw?"

"Yeah you shanked it."

"No… no I mean, my range finder, it was floating!"

"No. I did see that nice bird though."

*** ah hah hah ha ***

Plumb Bob Millionaire

I was having a terrible time in the mountains trying to read the greens. My friend Joey taught me how to plumb-bob a putt. It's a good technique if used at the right time. It's a terrible thing to teach someone who already has a lengthy routine. I taught this by mistake to Bob. Bob likes to say smell the roses as he walks around the entire green looking for the "flow". The flow is that portion of the green where the water runs off. Putts, as Bob will tell you, will run off in that direction.

Just before he plumb bobs, he looks at this watch. It's a solid gold Rolex Presidential. Bob has every gadget. I wondered whether he sent his watch away to James Bond and had Q add a "green reader" to it. For all of the calculations Bob requires, he waits. Bob does not look at the green or any of its topography until it's his turn.

"It's rude to be moving while someone is putting." Bob said while re-plumb-bobs his plumb-bob.

** Rude! How about being two holes behind the group in front of you? **

The Gimme Guy

I moved to Melbourne Beach and joined two leagues. We play the ball down here and we always putt out. That was not always the case in my men's clubs in the past. There is a belief that gimmes speed up the game. I say maybe but I doubt it. Too much discussion never sped this game up. One thing for sure; this is not how the game should be played.

I have missed my share of 6 inch putts. The time it takes to tap in a six inch putt or pick it up is negligible. Then you've always got the dilemma of the gimme distance. Some of these clubs have a two-foot gimme range. If you have a field of players, the gimme distance in one group may be different.

You've got to love George Buttlicker; he putts a short one, misses it and says, "Ah that was good; it was a gimme anyway?" A few holes later when you have the same distance Buttlicker jumps in and says, "You need to putt that one out; we've got to protect the field, you know!"

There are a lot of ways to speed this game up but this one has no merit. When you have to putt out there is no argument.

** It's certainly no gimme when you are still away. **

Storm a Brewing

The PGA and the LPGA commercials are getting into the spirit of faster play. It is not about playing fast it is just that playing slow is about poor planning, poor execution and the inability to reason or care. Mostly slow play is about absolute and positive stupidity. Pace is important for good rhythm and, because God has his own plans, a fast pace may be important to beat the weather.

There's a storm brewing and you've been waiting on every hole since number 2 and now you are in the fairway on 16. Clouds are coming in and then finally on number 18 the group in front of you finally speeds up and gets into the clubhouse just before you got soaking wet.

"Looks like you guys were a moment too late." One of them says as you drip on the clubhouse floor.

I think if the slow group in front of you gets in bone dry and your group got soaking wet there should be a penalty. You and your group should be allowed to stand on their table and pour their beer all over them.

** And you should be allowed to pass it through your kidneys first. **

8: Get to Know Jack

Jack

It does not matter that you cannot hear Jack; it is more about listening anyway. You cannot hit a good shot unless you can picture it in your mind. So Jack is always there to remind me of the *possibilities* of failure; but that is all in fun. Jack needles us and so does golf. If you can take a little of what is dealt to you, you'll be better company.

** You might even play better. **

"Really, Jack? You? Encouragement!?"

** Sorry, I got wrapped up in the moment. **

Needles and Pins

"I got wrapped up in the moment." That is how actors motivate themselves into the characters they play. A round of golf is like an episode on TV and the club is like a TV series. The show is only as good as its characters. Your character is how you carry yourself around the course. This determines whether someone wants to see you again or change the channel.

When I moved to Melbourne Beach I joined a few men's clubs in search of "a game" because that is what my friend Bob had told me to do.

** Ah, if you only had a brain. **

Each week I floated around from group to group and finally came to rest with three new amigos. In our foursome we have a bunch of average guys with common interests. Harry and I are shorter and younger. Harry has dark hair and his elbows stick out like a gunslinger. But it is not his gun you need to fear; it is his wit. No matter how good or bad you are playing Harry will bring you back to earth. We call him Needles because, when needed, Doctor Harry will give you a shot in the arm or other body part as prescribed.

There are a number of phrases you hear on the golf course and they seem to run a common theme. Bad shots are followed by "Why me?" These questions are rhetorical and only meant to share your frustration with the Man upstairs. But if Harry is in your company this is what is known to him as "an opportunity". Opportunities like this cannot dangle in the air unanswered.

"Why you? Probably because you are one of God's *special* people."

** Oh I've pointed that out so many times. **

Peter is a retired Rhode Island school teacher. He was an English teacher and you know what that means; he is highly intelligent and he sucks at math. Peter is tall with a full head of silver hair. Peter and Bill share a cart each week.

Bill brought his big smile from Michigan. Here in Florida, Michigan is a good place to be 'from'. Being from Michigan also allows you to pronounce the letter "R". He's the oldest of the group but still has all of his hair and it's still black. He loves the game like the rest of us and we discuss this friendly game in our foursome. We love the game but mostly we look forward to a few beers afterward.

We were on the practice green when he held out his new putter with a bit of pride.

"I am thinking that this is really going to help my game." Peter said as he drained three short ones.

"If it floats maybe Wayne will buy one." a well-used comment but Harry sounds like Joe Pesci with a New England accent; so we had to laugh.

There is an order of things in the world and scientists often explain them away but others remain a mystery. Right from the very first meeting Peter teed off first, I was second, then Bill and then Harry. If a fairway was a map of the United States, Harry's tee ball would start over the California coast then it would take the red-eye to Manhattan. I've never seen anything go from that far left to the far right since those protestors in the 60's joined the Republican Party. Still he manages to play this high banana with some degree of accuracy.

In the many rounds we have played this year we all seem to hit our ball into the same trouble spots. I mean we each have our own. I believe that bad memories have a profound impact on the golfer.

** I don't know how you possibly can count them all. **
"Thanks for support, Jack."
** Anytime I can help; I'm here for you. **

As a point in fact it seems nearly impossible for Harry to hit the 4th fairway. Harry tees up his ball; I look over at Peter and Bill and I point to the water in "right field" like Babe Ruth. In this case I call it Aquatropy. It is not a word but it has a Latin derivative "aquatropic" meaning drawn to the water. Harry's intention is to take the ball down the left side toward the trees and let it drift back to the fairway but the golf gods have other plans for Harry's ball. No matter how far left he aims his tee shot it flies down the middle and slings itself right in to the Boston Harbor with the rest of the Tea Party. No matter, Bill has a long and expert retriever in hand which he took out during Harry's backswing.

But all is not bad we root for each other and "Nice pah." is a common phrase in our group. A little something I picked up while I was stuck in New Hampshire.

** Common? So pars are common? What group are you playing with? **

Harry and I share a cart so we can make fun of each other at close range. After about three miserable holes I teed up and snapped hooked my ball toward the cart path.

"Don't hit the path, don't hit path, god damn it don't hit the path.!! And my voice trailed off as I added, "It hit the path!"

"Incredible. Maybe you should try yelling, "don't hit the fairway"."

That reminds me, playing with Harry is like having a real-life Jack around. Harry finds his ball in the rocks by the water.

"I think I can hit it but I might damage a club. Pass me your sand wedge."

* Back up a minute! What do you mean by real-life Jack? *

Bill thought out loud, "What do I need to get over the water here?"

"I think a raft and a bucket of range balls would do the trick."

Leaving yourself wide open for a good Harry comment is contagious. I was toying with getting on this par five in two

"Those guys are still on the green. I'm not sure whether to go for it or not." I said out loud before I could catch myself.

"Well you can either wait until they leave and top it half way down the fairway or hit it now and shank a lay-up into the water."

After I shanked the lay-up I turned to Harry, "What the hell is wrong with me today?"

"At least you didn't hit it far enough to go into the water... not yet anyway."

* Too bad. I really liked that shot before you hit it. *

"I don't think I could possibly play any worse."

"Oh, don't say that; there's a lot more holes left."

My ball had jumped into the rough but as we turned the corner I saw some glimmer of good fortune.

"It looks like I went into the rough but I can still see it so I probably have a good lie." I said.

"Then there's a good chance it's not your ball."

It wasn't my ball.

"I seem to have a group of bad shots followed by a good one; so I am overdo."

"You're probably right but then again, it could just be the start of another bad-shot grouping."

I managed to get out of the rough over the palms and somewhere near the green. As we drove up I said. "I see two balls up there. One's on the fringe and one's in the bunker."

"Based on your luck so far what are the odds of you being on the fringe?"

*** How does he do it? ***

"Does he remind you of anyone, Jack?"

*** Not sure, but there is something very likeable about this guy. ***

After the round we put away our clubs and met back in the bar for a few beers. Peter bought the first pitcher and was pouring as he spoke. "I just took a lesson and I think the guy totally screwed me up."

"He was your math teacher too, right?"

"No, I mean, I am so screwed up from that golf lesson I can't even remember my normal swing."

"Maybe I can go to that guy; I'd like to forget your normal swing." Harry drank a little wine and then put the glass down, "I wish I took this game up when I was younger."

Peter calculated. "That would probably double your life-to-date lost ball count."

This becomes a habit but one thing I can say for sure, we all enjoy a good shot and we really do root for each other's success.

** Good shots are special because of their rarity. **

The Best Medicine

Jack and I joined another group closer to home on Mondays and Thursdays.

** Nice of you to let me tag along. **

"Did I have a choice?"

** Not really. **

When you play during the week you find almost all of the guys are retired. I hooked up with a couple of Red Sox fans. They had not retired from that apparently.

** Missing New Hampshire, are we? **

I realized that snide comments tossed out at the right moment annoys some people. It's not so bad though; I don't get to play with them more than once. My terrible shots usually come in three's. This is a good time to make fun of yourself; I find it helps a great deal. Your partners laugh a lot harder.

** And the tears are then mistaken for joy. **

As a golfer Barry is an ex-marine mostly. This means he's going to smack the ball into submission right off the tee. He gets to the green in two and he lines up for a nine foot birdie putt which he leaves short.

He yells "Hit the ball you dumb ass!"

Tony turns and says, "It's not my turn yet."

We all got a kick out of that. Tony looks like a character right out of the movies. His dark hair covers thick tanned arms. He's stocky and he looks like he needs a shave after he just took a shave.

"Did you hear that Tony's suing the city of Melbourne?" Gene asked.

"No."

"They built the sidewalks too close to his ass."

Gene left the seminary before becoming a priest. He found women far too interesting and actually married one. I guess that happens sometimes.

*** Maybe not as often as it should. ***

If Tony is Italian then Gene is just as Irish. He paints shamrocks on his ball with a Sharpie.

"What are you writing there Gene, a farewell message?"

"That's too funny. I bet there are a lot of shamrocks in these trees." Gene smiled.

"I've donated my fair share."

*** Oh the day ain't over yet. ***

We all grew up Catholic and getting away with a snicker or a laugh is inbred in us all. We were standing on the first tee taking a few practice swings. Gene stopped his swing at the top for a moment.

214

"I just checked my backswing at the top and you know what I noticed."

"You have two hands and you have a glove on one of them." Barry said.

"Yeah, that's what I was thinking." Gene realized the absurdity of it all.

When we got to the sixteenth Tony and I both hit our tee shots in the woods. Tony's popped out and mine did not.

"How come when you hit a ball in the woods it pops out and when I hit one in the woods it stays in there."

"I'm guessing that you're just one of God's *special* people."

"Do you know Jack?"

"Jack who?"

Even Quitting Takes Practice

Some of our best shots come when we don't really care. We drain a six foot putt that doesn't matter or hit a perfect lay-up on a par five. This justifies everything Jack said about frustration and replacing high expectations with low goals.

** Excuse me? **

"You were right all along Jack. It's not about expectations but it *is* about being good company. I know, I have some anger management issues of my own. I have been bad company."

** Finally. **

It takes great practice to turn anger into laughter. When I am able to laugh at myself with the other golfers then they will seek me for *a game*. When I enjoy the company all of those little tirades disappear. If you do then all of those little asterisks may vanish for you...

...and then you will know me, Jack La Merde.

You decide.

Before I forget I just wanted to thank all of these characters for putting their Foot-joys in their beer hole for our entertainment.

The End

Hi… Jack here! There's an empty trash can just waiting for you.

Bibliography

(Alphabetical by name as mentioned in book.)

I would like to extend my thanks to Google, the International Movie Database (IMDB) and Wikipedia for their help in my research and completion of the credits/bibliography.

The **Addams Family** (TV 1964-6) was about a satirical eccentric, wealthy clan who delights in the macabre and they are unaware that people find them bizarre or frightening. Lurch was the overly tall and pale butler.

Alice in Wonderland – reference was made to the huge smile of the Cheshire Cat in Walt Disney's 1951 animated version of Alice in Wonderland. Alice's Adventures in Wonderland is an 1865 novel written by English author Charles Lutwidge Dodgson under the pseudonym Lewis Carroll. It was published in 1865.

Arnold Schwarzenegger (born 07/30/1947) is an Austrian and former professional bodybuilder, actor, producer, director, businessman, investor, and politician.

Arnold Daniel Palmer, Nicknamed "The King," (born 09/10/1929) is an American professional golfer, is generally regarded as one of the greatest players in history.

Art Carney – (1918- 2003) "Art" Carney was an American actor in film, stage, television and radio. He is best known for playing Ed Norton, opposite Jackie Gleason's Ralph Kramden in the situation comedy. He made a point to overdo a pre-routine such as wiping a page with the back of his hand again, again and again before signing?

Babe Ruth - George Herman **"Babe" Ruth,** Jr. (February 6, 1895 – August 16, 1948) was an American professional baseball player. He helped the Yankees win seven pennants and four World Series titles. Ruth retired in 1935 after a short stint with the Boston Braves, and the following year, he became one of the first five players to be elected into the National Baseball Hall of Fame.

Bilbo Baggins – is the title character and protagonist of J. R. R. Tolkien's 1937 novel *The Hobbit.* **Hobbits** are fictional diminutive hairy humanoid races that inhabit the lands of middle-earth in Tolkien's fiction.

Brian Keith (November 14, 1921 – June 24, 1997) was a broad shouldered 6'1" American film star (The Parent Trap), television star (Family Affair), and stage actor who had Irish good looks.

Caddy Shack – 1980 film directed by Harold Ramis - Amusing movie about a golf course and the characters that play on it. Rodney Dangerfield has a line, "While we're still young!" that he yells to the slow group in front of him to get them moving.

City Slickers - 1991 American comedy film directed by Ron Underwood. This references a scene where Curly, played by Jack Palance, was asked if had killed anyone today. Curly simply replied, "The day ain't over yet."

Cheech Marin - Richard Anthony "Cheech" Marin is a smiling round faced Mexican American comedian, actor and writer who gained recognition as part of the comedy act Cheech & Chong during the 1970s and other TV rolls.

A **Clockwork Orange** is a 1971 film written, directed and produced by Stanley Kubrick. In futuristic Britain, juvenile delinquents volunteer for an experimental aversion therapy to solve their crime problem but not all goes to plan.

Dennis the Menace, Hank Ketcham created a comic strip character who was precocious but lovable, freckle-faced five-and-a-half-year-old boy with a famous blond cowlick and a penchant for mischief.

Dorian Gray – Oscar Wilde authored "The Picture of Dorian Gray" about an artist who painted a picture of Dorian. Dorian curses his portrait, which he believes will one day remind him of the beauty he will one day have lost. In a fit of distress, he pledges his soul if only the painting could bear the burden of age and infamy, allowing him to stay forever young.

Foot Joy – Foot Joy is a brand name of a leading manufacturer of golf shoes.

Foster Brooks – (1912 – 2001) American comedian whose act was a lovable drunk who stumbled over his words.

Gary Player – (born 1935) is a South African professional golfer, regarded as one of the greatest players in the history of golf. Player accumulated an impressive nine major championships on the regular tour At the age 29, Player won the 1965 U.S. Open and became the only non-American to win all four majors, known as the career Grand Slam.

George Michael Steinbrenner III was an American businessman who was the principal owner and managing partner of Major League Baseball's New York Yankees.

Gibbs - Special Agent Leroy Jethro Gibbs is a character from NCIS. He makes up humorous yet sensible rules to be followed and assigns a number to each one. NCIS is an American police drama television series on CBS, revolving around a fictional team of special agents from the Naval Criminal Investigative Service.

Holmes, Sherlock – A brilliant fictional detective created by writer Sir Arthur Canon Doyle. Holmes could see and solve mysteries others could not.

Jack is a fictional character who speaks but is usually only heard by me (in italics). He is my close personal inner conscience and tormenter throughout the book.

James Bond and Q – In 1953 author Ian Fleming created a British super spy named James Bond, code named 007. Bond was often outfitted with spy gadgetry by an engineer simply known as "Q".

Jimmy Demaret - James Newton Demaret was an American professional golfer. He won 31 PGA Tour events in a long career between 1935 and 1957, and was the first three-time winner of the Masters, with titles in 1940, 1947, and 1950.

Joe Pesci - Joseph Frank "Joe" Pesci is an American actor, comedian and musician, known for playing tough, volatile characters, in a variety of genres.

John William "Johnny" Carson (October 23, 1925 – January 23, 2005) was a dark haired, slim American comedian and most renowned television host for thirty years.

Ken Venturi – (1931-2013) a well-travelled American professional golfer and CBS broadcaster who won 14 events including the US Open in 1964. He loved Ireland especially the course at LaHinch.

Leslie William Nielsen, (2/11/1926 – 11/28/2010) was a prematurely grey actor and comedian. He received positive reviews as a serious actor although he is primarily known for his comedic roles in 1980s and 90s in *The Naked Gun* film series, and *Police Squad!*

Lee Trevino – A Mexican-American PGA professional golfer who is known for his colorful quips and humor.

Lewis Black is a brilliantly raw comedian who finds humor in the absolute truth. I refer to his explanation on golf and golfers.

Lizzy Borden - *Lizzie* Andrew *Borden* (July 19, 1860 – June 1, 1927) was an American woman who was tried and acquitted in the 1892 axe murders of her father and mother. It was said that she "Gave her mother 40 whacks…gave her father 41."

Lou Costello - Louis Francis "Lou" Costello (March 6, 1906 – March 3, 1959) was an American actor and comedian best remembered for the comedy double act of Abbott and Costello, with Bud Abbott.

NCIS (September 2003 to present) is a CBS television series, revolving around a fictional team of special agents from the Naval Criminal Investigative Service, The show was created by Donald Bellisario, Don McGill.

Richard Branson is the owner of Virgin Atlantic Airlines.

Rod Serling - see Twilight Zone below.

Rodney Dangerfield – see Caddy Shack above.

Shakespeare, William – (1564-1616) was an English poet and playwright, widely regarded as the greatest writer in the English language and the world's pre-eminent dramatist. He is often called England's national poet and the "Bard of Avon".

Silence of the Lambs - is a 1991 American thriller film that blends elements of the crime and horror genres. It was directed by Jonathan Demme and stars Jodie Foster, Anthony Hopkins, Ted Levine, and Scott Glenn.

Tom Hanks – (Born July 9, 1956) Thomas Jeffrey "Tom" Hanks is an American actor, producer, writer, and director. Hanks is best known for his roles in Big, A League of Their Own, Sleepless in Seattle, Forrest Gump, Apollo 13.

Tiger Woods "Tiger" Woods is an American professional golfer whose achievements to date rank him among the most successful golfers of all time. He is also one of the longest hitters in the game of golf.

Truman, Harry S. – 33rd President of the United States from 1945 to 1953.

Twilight Zone was an American television series on CBS from 1959 to 1964. It dealt mostly with supernatural and fictional events. It was created and narrated by writer Rod Serling

USGA - One of the core functions of the USGA (United States Golf Association) is to write and interpret the Rules of Golf. The Association does this in conjunction with the R&A in St. Andrews, Scotland.

Winston Churchill said "Golf is a game whose aim is to hit a very small ball into an even smaller hole, with weapons singularly ill-designed for the purpose."

Yogi Berra - Lawrence Peter "Yogi" Berra (born 05/12/ 1925) was a former Major League Baseball catcher (1946–1965) for the NY Yankees. He has a tendency toward clever quips. "It ain't over 'til it's over" is arguably his most famous example and often quoted.

Author's Bio

Wayne Martin authors humorous memoirs that capture life's moments. He is politically incorrect and only an innuendo away from his blatant truth. Your own reflections will come to life allowing a laugh at these characters and their misadventures.

Wayne has utilized his humor in speaking engagements in the U.S. from NY to Hawaii; and internationally to India and even to Miami (which, according to the street signs, is no longer part of the U.S.).

Also by this Author

"Confessions of an Altar Boy"

Humorous memoirs of a band of less than well-behaved students in an otherwise strict parochial school (circa 1950s-60s).

Review - 5 stars

"I enjoyed both bursts of laughter and sweet nostalgia. Mr. Martin's writing reeled me in to the parochial school setting of St. Mary's...The antics of friends and altar boys ... literally had me laughing out loud."

- MG413at
Amazon.com

Review - 5 stars

"I loved it! ... I found myself laughing out loud and also being transported back in time...I enjoyed every page and every daydream as told through the eyes of this very talented writer who lived it himself. What a fun story and much appreciated walk down memory lane!"

- MJ Butler, Author
"A New Year's Eve to Remember"

ISBN 978-1484969267

Made in the USA
Charleston, SC
14 January 2014